TRACING YOUR
family history
IN HERTFORDSHIRE

L'

TRACING YOUR
family history
IN HERTFORDSHIRE

*Hertfordshire Archives
and Local Studies (HALS)*

*Monumental brass of William Chapman
(died 1621) and his family from Walkern Church
(Ref. Oldfield Vol 6)*

HERTFORDSHIRE PUBLICATIONS
*An imprint of the
University of Hertfordshire Press*

First published in Great Britain in 2003 by
Hertfordshire Publications

an imprint of the
University of Hertfordshire Press
Learning and Information Services
University of Hertfordshire
College Lane,
Hatfield,
Hertfordshire AL10 9AB

*Hertfordshire Publications, an imprint of the
University of Hertfordshire Press, is published on behalf of
the Hertfordshire Association for Local History*

ISBN 0 9542189 2 2

British Library Cataloguing in Publication Data.
A catalogue record for this book is available from the British Library

Design by Whiteing Design Partnership, Hemel Hempstead HP2 7SX
Cover design by John Robertshaw, Harpenden AL5 2JB
Printed in Great Britain by Antony Rowe Ltd., Chippenham SN14 6LH

Contents

Acknowledgements

This book has had many contributors, mainly past and present members of HALS' staff, including: Sue Flood, Christine Shearman, Jeremy McIlwaine, Dr Kate Thompson, Samantha McNeilly, Nick Connell, Eileen Wallace, Ruth Pyle, and Amanda Johnston. Other staff have been involved in other ways, including Dr Jill Barber who assisted with editorial reading, and Di Vanderson who assisted with the selection and scanning of the illustrations.

We are also most grateful to Sharon Floate for her contribution on Gypsy and Traveller ancestors, to Ken Griffin for his contribution on transportation, and to the other members of the editorial committee of Hertfordshire Publications – Dr Nigel Goose, Dr Gillian Gear, and Bill Forster – for their helpful suggestions and corrections, and support throughout.

But without doubt the greatest burden of work fell to Margaret Ward, whose 'editing' work for HALS extended far beyond editing and involved much rewriting and writing of new material. To her we owe our deepest gratitude and sincere praise for bringing this book finally to fruition; for her patience and good humour throughout, and for doing such an excellent job. Her knowledge as a family historian combined with her skills as a writer and editor proved ideal and it has been a pleasure to work with her.

Christine Shearman
On behalf of Hertfordshire Archives & Local Studies
and Hertfordshire Publications

Introduction

This practical and comprehensive guide provides an introduction to everything family historians need to know to begin tracing their Hertfordshire ancestors. The information that appeared in Genealogical Sources (Hertfordshire Record Office, 1987) has been completely revised and updated, and considerably expanded, to offer a new generation of family historians a source of reference and information. It provides invaluable information both to those researching locally and those searching from a distance; relevant web sites are quoted throughout the text.

The book is thematic in approach, the chapters incorporating related material on subjects as broad as military ancestors and the poor and the sick. Every aspect of our ancestors' lives has been considered, from their birth and baptism to their death and burial.

In each chapter a brief background to the subject is followed by a description of the kinds of records you can expect to find, including their usefulness to family historians, and an indication of where those records are held. The emphasis is on sources available in Hertfordshire, and particularly those held at Hertfordshire Archives and Local Studies (HALS), but where useful records are known to be held elsewhere this is noted in the text. Catalogue references are given in brackets, e.g. (HALS: DP/21/1), making it simple to find the original documents referred to. Some suggestions for further reading are also given which will help to fill in background information or indicate where other records can be found.

Appendices have been used to provide useful addresses and websites, and also to list in detail the availability of essential sources such as parish registers, nonconformist registers and the whereabouts of wills before 1858.

Family historians who live in Hertfordshire but are researching ancestors from other counties are not forgotten. The availability of the International Genealogical Index (IGI), indexes to the registers of births, marriages and deaths since 1837, indexes to post-1858 wills and many other national resources held locally are covered in the appropriate chapters.

It would be beyond the scope of any one book to list every document held at HALS which might be of interest and help to an individual researcher. It is hoped, however, that with the information given here, family historians will be encouraged to delve deeper into the catalogues, making their own discoveries with each new connection uncovered.

Hertfordshire Archives and Local Studies (HALS)

Hertfordshire Archives and Local Studies is the joint county record office and local studies library for the county, a part of the County Council based at County Hall in Hertford. HALS provides archive and library services to anyone interested in the history of Hertfordshire and its inhabitants. Books, pamphlets, photographs, maps, newspapers and original documents (dating from 1060 to the present day) are preserved here, and many of the sources most useful to family historians are increasingly available on microfilm or fiche in the Family History Centre, making them easy and convenient to use.

Visitors using the Family History Centre at Hertfordshire Archives & Local Studies (HALS).

Computer and Internet facilities are also available. HALS' Family History Centre is quite separate from and not to be confused with the 'Family History Centres' of the Church of the Latter Day Saints (see page 4).

Much of the material at HALS is unique and irreplaceable and for this reason you are asked to observe a few simple rules which will be explained to you on arrival.

To use the microfilm or microfiche readers in the Family History Centre (for which there is a charge), you are advised to book beforehand. You can book using the website, or by telephone.

If you wish to use original archives, you will need a County Archive Research Network (CARN) card. This can be issued immediately if you can provide two pieces of identification, one bearing your name and address and the other your signature.

Please note that documents required for Tuesday evenings and Saturdays must be ordered in advance. Documents may not be ordered between 12.15 - 2.00 pm or during the last hour before closing.

If you cannot undertake your research personally, HALS offers a postal research service. For further details of services, access arrangements and current charges, please contact HALS or visit the website: <www.hertsdirect.org/hals>. See Appendix VI for full contact details.

Hertfordshire's libraries and museums

Some material relevant to tracing family history is available at main libraries throughout Hertfordshire, mainly in the form of the International Genealogical Index (IGI) and filmed census returns and parish registers. Many libraries also hold nineteenth century directories and other printed material that will be useful to family historians. An indication of current holdings is given in Appendix V, and up to date information can be had from the appropriate library or from the website.

When searching for a particular book, it is easy to check its whereabouts in the county by using the on-line library catalogue at <www.hertsdirect.org/libraries> (ask library staff for details if you do not have access to a computer). Most books can be ordered through the inter-library loan system.

There may also be background material to be found at museums, especially about the area in which your ancestor lived. A list of Hertfordshire's museums is given in Appendix VI.

Charles and Isobel Ashford and their children of Brocket Lodge, Hoddesdon, c1900 (Lowewood Museum, Borough of Broxbourne).

Hertfordshire Family History Society

Hertfordshire Family History Society was founded in 1977 and plays a leading role in genealogical research in the county. It welcomes new members, whether beginners or experienced researchers, and has a varied programme of talks which are of interest to all family historians, whether they have Hertfordshire connections or not; search services and research facilities are also available. The society is involved in many county transcription and indexing projects (referred to in the appropriate chapters) and has a wide range of publications. For more information contact the society by e-mail at <secretary@hertsfhs.org.uk>, or see their website at <www.hertsfhs.org.uk>.

LDS Family History Centres

The Church of Jesus Christ of Latter-day Saints (LDS or Mormons) runs a number of Family History Centres in the UK and abroad which are open to all family historians. It is possible to order films of parish registers, census returns and other material through the centres, to be viewed there, and to consult the full range of LDS sources. Details of what has been microfilmed and can be consulted in LDS Family History Centres can be seen in the Family History Library Catalog which has been published on CD-ROM and can also be accessed on the web at <www.familysearch.org/>. See Appendix VI for addresses and contact telephone numbers in Hertfordshire.

Chapter 1

The administrative background

It will be helpful for family historians to know something of the administrative structure of Hertfordshire in the past, as this could have affected where records were held, whether they have survived and how they may be arranged today.

Hundreds

Hundreds are subdivisions of the county, created before the Norman Conquest for local government purposes, with judicial, financial and military responsibilities. Taxes such as the hearth tax, for instance, and military records such as muster rolls or militia lists may be found among the records of the hundreds. This system continued until well into the 1800s and so knowing which hundred your ancestor's parish was in will sometimes be a shortcut to finding the relevant records or background information – nineteenth-century county histories, for instance, usually describe parishes collected together within their hundreds.

Hertfordshire has eight hundreds – Braughing, Broadwater, Cashio, Dacorum, Edwinstree, Hertford, Hitchin (half-hundred) and Odsey (see map, pages 6-7). Although the area controlled by the hundred court is usually a recognisably compact entity, in Dacorum, Cashio (see below) and Broadwater there were a few outlying parishes, which may lead to confusion if not noted.

The Liberty of St Albans

A liberty was an area that was outside the jurisdiction of the sheriff of the county. The Liberty of St Albans was made up of the lands originally under the control of the Abbey of St Alban; after the dissolution of the abbey in 1539, the liberty continued to be treated separately from the county until 1874 and had its own court of quarter sessions.

HERTFORDSHIRE
Hundreds and Parishes

HUNDREDS
1. ODSEY
2. HITCHIN
3. BROADWATER
4. EDWINSTREE
5. BRAUGHING
6. DACORUM
7. CASHIO
8. HERTFORD

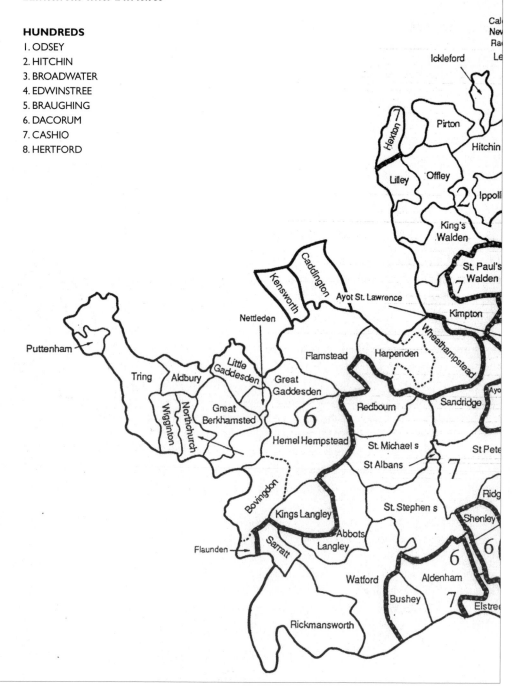

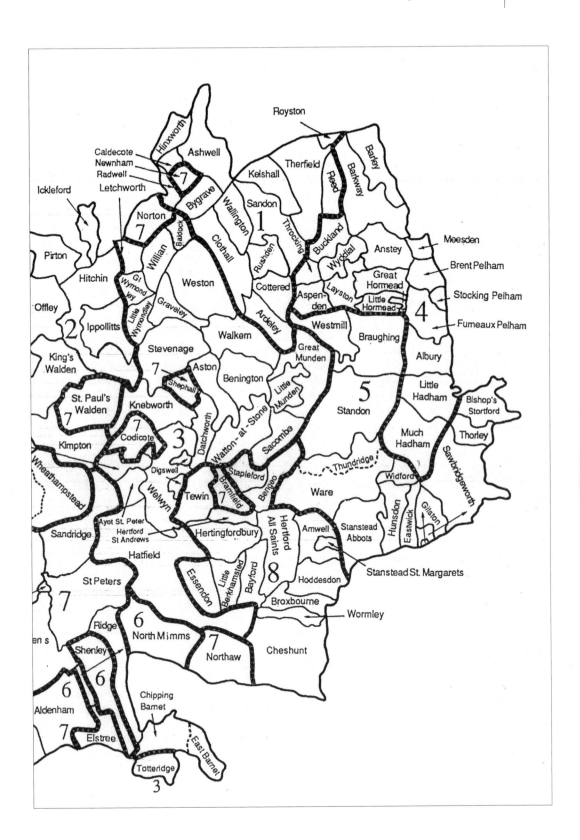

Ecclesiastical Administration:
where to find wills

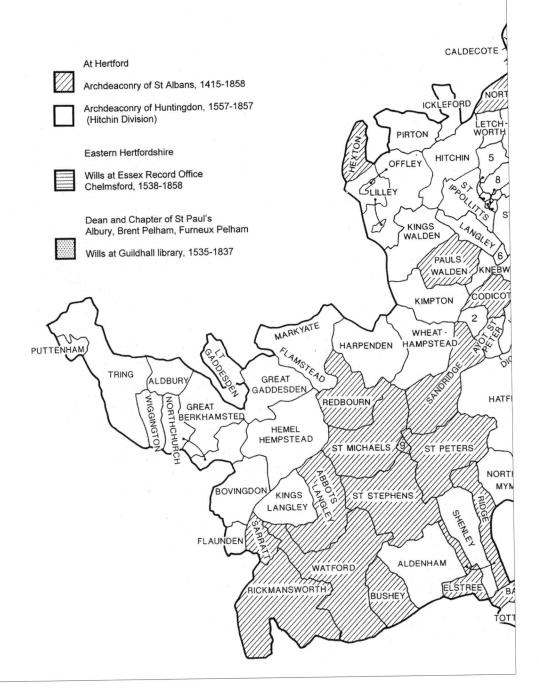

At Hertford

Archdeaconry of St Albans, 1415-1858

Archdeaconry of Huntingdon, 1557-1857
(Hitchin Division)

Eastern Hertfordshire

Wills at Essex Record Office
Chelmsford, 1538-1858

Dean and Chapter of St Paul's
Albury, Brent Pelham, Furneux Pelham

Wills at Guildhall library, 1535-1837

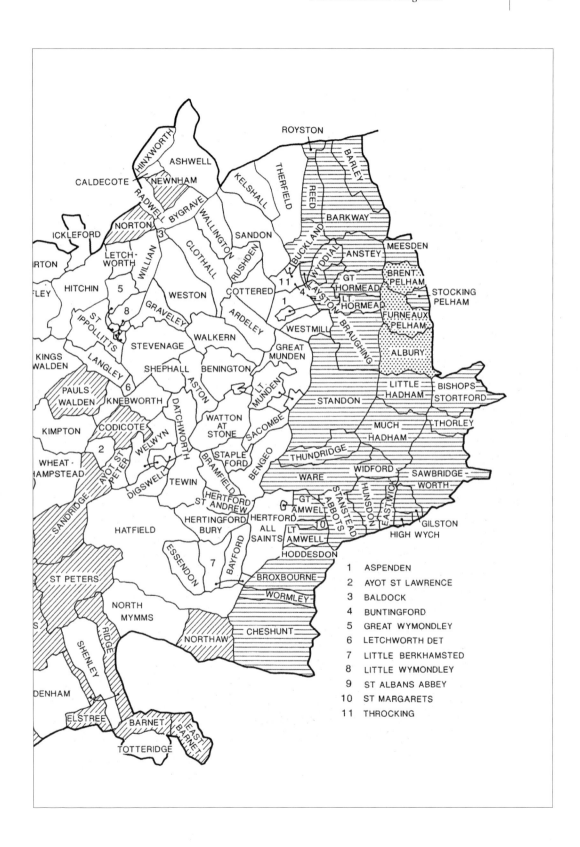

1   ASPENDEN
2   AYOT ST LAWRENCE
3   BALDOCK
4   BUNTINGFORD
5   GREAT WYMONDLEY
6   LETCHWORTH DET
7   LITTLE BERKHAMSTED
8   LITTLE WYMONDLEY
9   ST ALBANS ABBEY
10 ST MARGARETS
11 THROCKING

Poor Law Unions and Registration Districts

1 Royston
2 Hitchin
3 Buntingford
4 Bishops Stortford
5 Ware
6 Hertford
7 Welywn (combined with Hatfield 1921)
8 Edmonton (records held at London Metropolitan Archives)
9 Hatfield (combined with Welwyn 1921)
10 St Albans
11 Hemel Hempstead
12 Berkhamsted
13 Watford
14 Barnet

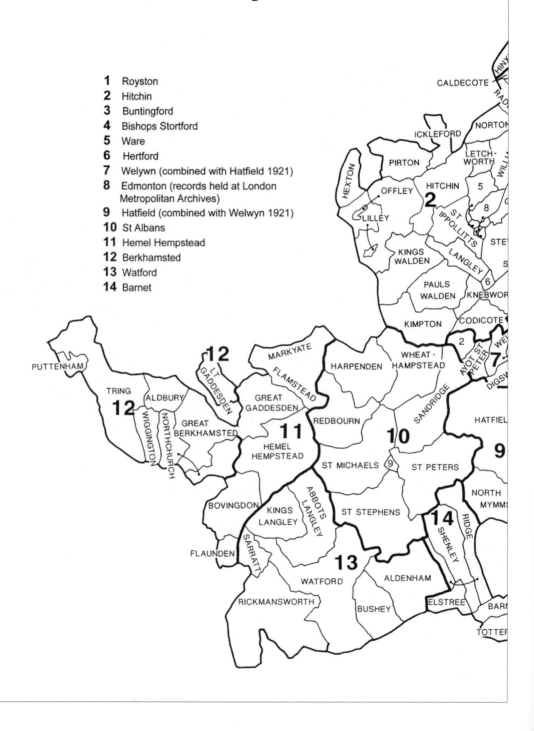

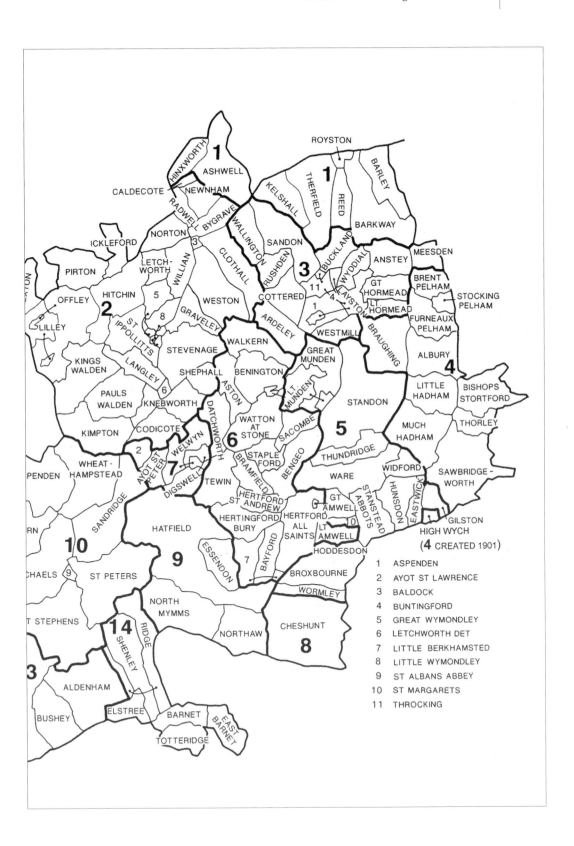

The hundred of Cashio encompassed the parishes contained within the liberty. These were the four parishes covering the town of St Albans and most of the parishes south of it to the Middlesex border, together with seven other parishes to the north, some quite detached from this geographical block, and Northaw to the east; there were also four Buckinghamshire parishes. Family historians should note that ancestors guilty of crimes quite remote from the town of St Albans may nevertheless have been brought before the liberty court held there.

Ecclesiastical administration

Today Hertfordshire comes within the Diocese of St Albans, with the two archdeaconries of St Albans and Bedford covering roughly the same areas as the counties of Hertfordshire and Bedfordshire. This comparative simplicity conceals a past ecclesiastical history of extraordinary complexity. For the family historian this is of interest because in the past the church courts handled a great deal of business which affected our ancestors' lives. Wills proved before 1858, bishops' transcripts and marriage licences are just a few of the records that were originally kept by the appropriate diocese. (see map, pages 8-9)

Before 1845 Hertfordshire lay within three different archdeaconries and was divided between two large and powerful dioceses, London and Lincoln. The old Archdeaconry of St Albans was made up of the parishes contained within the Liberty of St Albans (see above). Until the dissolution of the abbey it had owed no allegiance to any diocesan bishop, but in 1550 it was annexed to the Diocese of London. The diocese also controlled, through the Archdeaconry of Middlesex (Essex and Herts. division), all the parishes east of an approximate north to south line from Royston to Cheshunt. There were a few exceptions within that area – three parishes that were peculiars (meaning simply that they were exempt from the jurisdiction of the appropriate diocese) of the Dean and Chapter of St Paul's and five which for purposes of probate of wills came under the jurisdiction of either the Consistory or the Commissary Courts of the Bishops of London. The rest of the county, the main central block and the west, formed the Hitchin division of the Archdeaconry of Huntingdon, which was in the Diocese of Lincoln.

Rationalisation of this complicated situation took place in 1845 when the Archdeaconry of St Albans was reconstructed to include the whole county; the four Buckinghamshire parishes were transferred to the Diocese of Oxford at this point. This new archdeaconry was assigned to the Diocese of Rochester. In 1877 the new Diocese of St Albans was established, covering the archdeaconries of St Albans, Essex, Colchester and part of Kent but in 1914 the diocese was given its present structure.

Parishes

The parish is the smallest of the ancient ecclesiastical administrative units, defined by its parish church and an incumbent licensed to perform religious services, including baptisms, marriages and burials, within the established Church of England. From Tudor times, the civil parish (the boundaries of which invariably followed those of the ecclesiastical parish) also had functions to perform, such as the administration of the poor law. The parish is, therefore, the source of much of the information a family historian will seek.

There are 132 ancient parishes in Hertfordshire (see map, pages 6-7). During the nineteenth and twentieth centuries, with a growing population, some of these were subdivided and either new churches built or existing chapels of ease given full parish status. (See also *Boundary and civil parish changes,* below.)

Poor Law Unions and Registration Districts

Under the 1834 Poor Law Amendment Act, parishes were grouped together as unions, run by elected boards of guardians. The workhouse would draw its inmates from all the parishes within that union. The boundaries of the unions were then largely used in the creation of registration districts when the civil registration system commenced in 1837. These districts extended in some cases over the county boundary. (see map, pages 10-11)

Boundary and civil parish changes

Hertfordshire's boundaries have been 'tidied up' at times in the past which resulted in a small number of parishes being transferred into, or out of, the county. See Appendix I, and relevant chapters, for notes about where to find the records for these parishes. The changes, and the creation and abolition of *civil parishes,* are briefly as follows (dates for creation of ecclesiastical parishes will be found in Appendix I):

1894   Bengeo divided, part to Hertford, part to create Bengeo Rural; Langley, Preston, St Michael Rural, St Peter Rural, St Stephen Rural, Tring Rural, Ware Rural, Watford Rural created.

1895   Nettleden transferred to Hertfordshire from Buckinghamshire.

1897   Holwell transferred to Hertfordshire from Bedfordshire; Kensworth, Caddington and Studham transferred to Bedfordshire from Hertfordshire; Markyate created; Royston transferred completely into Hertfordshire from Cambridgeshire.

1898   Chorleywood and Harpenden Rural created.

1901   High Wych created.

1904   part of Monken Hadley transferred to Hertfordshire from Middlesex.

1908   Norton abolished at the formal creation of Letchworth Garden City.

1921   Welwyn Garden City created.

1935   Broxbourne, Digswell, Willian, Wormley abolished;
       Buntingford created.

1937   Great Hormead, Little Hormead, Great Wymondley, Little
       Wymondley, Layston abolished; Hormead, Nettleden with
       Potten End, Wymondley created.

1947   Colney Heath, London Colney created; St Peter Rural abolished.

1953   Shephall abolished.

1955   Broadfield, Throcking abolished.

1958   Chipperfield created.

1964   Puttenham abolished.

1965   Barnet, East Barnet and Totteridge transferred to Middlesex;
       Potters Bar, South Mimms transferred to Hertfordshire
       from Middlesex.

1974   Nash Mills created.

1986   Croxley Green created.

1990   Hertford Heath created (from Little Amwell and parts of
       other parishes); Little Amwell abolished.

Chapter 2

Births, marriages and deaths

From the sixteenth century to 1837 parish registers provide the only record of baptisms, marriages and burials for the majority of people in England and Wales. Despite their deficiencies and occasional gaps, these registers form the principal source for genealogical information over that period. In 1837 civil registration of births, marriages and deaths was introduced and the certificates that record these life events are normally the first major source family historians consult. This chapter looks at the background to both these important sources and their availability in Hertfordshire, and at other records that can provide more information about births, marriages and deaths.

Civil registration

When beginning to trace your family history, you should start with more recent events and work back through the years. Certificates of births, marriages and deaths are essential sources for this first step.

By the early nineteenth century, it was becoming apparent that the parish-based system of recording baptisms, marriages and burials was no longer adequate to provide an accurate picture of the rapidly increasing population. The rise of nonconformity and the huge growth of some industrial towns which had few Anglican churches, meant that fewer people were having these life events recorded by their local parish church. So in 1836 the Registration Act was passed, establishing the General Register Office (GRO) and making it a legal requirement to register all births, marriages and deaths. This act came into force on 1 July 1837. At the same time, the Marriages Act made it possible to contract a recognised civil marriage in a register office. The civil registration indexes, and the certificates themselves, will help to trace ancestors back to the early 1830s.

England and Wales were divided by the Act into registration districts (see map, pages 10-11). Births, marriages and deaths were now recorded by local registrars who issued a certificate of the event to those concerned and forwarded a copy to the superintendent registrar of the district. However, civil registration was unpopular in the early years and it is believed that a great many events went unrecorded. In 1874 the Births and Deaths Registration Act transferred the responsibility for registration from the registrar onto the persons present at a birth or death (usually family members), with a fine for late registration of births (after six weeks), thereby making registration compulsory. The records are therefore much fuller from 1875.

British subjects living abroad were also required to register births, marriages and deaths, and there is a range of these registers from British consulates and high commissions, varying in dates and formats. Births and deaths at sea in UK-registered ships were registered from 1837, much later extended to cover aircraft, hovercraft and off-shore installations. Deaths in the Boer War (1899-1902) and the two world wars are also recorded.

The GRO indexes

Superintendent registrars sent a copy of all certificates to the Registrar General at the GRO, where a quarterly index was prepared. The indexes are held in large bound volumes at the Family Records Centre (FRC) in London; the certificates themselves are at the Office for National Statistics (ONS) in Southport and the only way to access them is to apply there using the information provided by the indexes. However, the indexes have been copied and are widely available on microfiche at libraries and record offices all over the country, with national sets being held by larger centres. In Hertfordshire, a full set is held at HALS.

The indexes are alphabetical by surname, arranged by year and then in quarters. The March quarter covers all events registered from January to March; the June quarter from April to June; the September quarter from July to September; and the December quarter from October to December. The microfiche are colour-coded red for births, green for marriages and blue for deaths.

The appearance of the indexes has changed over the years, reflecting the technology of the times: hand-written from 1837 to 1866; printed (typeset) from 1866 to 1910; typed from 1910 to 1970; computer-generated from 1970; with annual rather than quarterly accumulations from 1984.

What the indexes tell you

Each of the indexes contains similar information: the surname and first name of the subject, the registration district where the event was registered (which may not necessarily be the exact town or village where it took place) and a volume and page number. From 1866 a second forename was also given in full but from July 1910 this was abbreviated to an initial only. Changes in the format of the indexes have occurred over the years:

- ◆ **Births:** from the September quarter 1911 the mother's maiden surname is given.
- ◆ **Marriages:** from the March quarter 1912 the surnames of both parties are shown.
- ◆ **Deaths:** from the March quarter 1866 the age at death is given, and from the June quarter 1969 the deceased's date of birth.

| | | | | | | | | | | | BAR-BAR |

BIRTHS REGISTERED IN JANUARY, FBERUARY, MARCH 1863

NAME		SUP-REGISTRARS DISTRICT	VOL	PAGE	NAME		SUP-REGISTRARS DISTRICT	VOL	PAGE
BARLOW	John James	Blackburn	8e	372	BARNARD	Elizabeth	Whitby	9d	397
	Sohn Samuel	Bury	8c	400		Elizabeth	Kensington	1a	2
	John Summerscales					Elizabeth Mary	Lambeth	1d	300
		Salford	8d	59		Ellingham	Frome	5c	613
	John Thomas	Basford	7b	79		Emily	Dunmow	4a	375
	John William	Manchester	8d	243		Francis George	Shoreditch	1c	121
	Joseph	Oldham	8d	536		Frederick	Woodbridge	4a	645
	Joseph	Salford	8d	17		Frederick	W Ham	4a	31
	Joseph	Bethnal Gn	1c	278		Frederick	Depwade	4b	234
	Joseph Entwisle	Bury	8c	421		Frederick John	Farnham	2a	78
	Joseph Henry	Stockport	8a	23		George	London City	1c	64
	Joseph Smith	Huddersfield	9a	309		George Alfred	Romford	4a	98
	Kershaw	Altrincham	8a	149		Hannah Jane	Hoo	2a	365
	Laura Bessie	Chipping N	3a	641		Henry James	Bristol	6a	11
	Lizzie	Chorlton	8c	656		James	Faversham	2a	674
	Louisa Alice	W Derby	8b	328		James William	Eastbourne	2b	53

It is important to record all the information given in an entry, including the year and quarter you found it in. Bear in mind that births and deaths may well appear in subsequent quarters as they could be registered up to six weeks after the event (and within six months on payment of a fine). Marriages, on the other hand, were registered on the day they took place. If you are unable to find a person, try looking under variations in spelling of the surname.

Extract from the microfiche indexes to births in England and Wales, March quarter 1863. Crown copyright - ONS - reproduced by permission of the controller of HMSO.

Obtaining certificates

Once you have identified an ancestor in the indexes you can proceed, for a fee, to obtain a copy certificate. This can be done, using the GRO reference, at the FRC in London, by completing a request form and paying over the counter. The certificate will normally be sent to your home address within a week. Alternatively, you can order by post direct from: The ONS (General Register Office, PO Box 2, Southport, Merseyside PR8 2JD), or by telephone (0870 243 77 88). See the ONS website at <www.statistics.gov.uk/registration/certificates.asp> for full details. When applying to the GRO, always quote exactly what appears in the indexes (including what you believe are errors!) as this is what will be used to locate the certificate.

If you are seeking a certificate for an event registered in Hertfordshire, it is possible to order it directly from the local superintendent registrar over the Internet, with secure online payment. Full details of the procedure are given at <www.hertsdirect.org>.

You can also contact register offices in other parts of the country; HALS holds a list of all the offices in England and Wales and can provide details. An increasing number of register offices are making local indexes and ordering procedures available over the Internet.

There are some occasions when a local register office may be unable to supply a marriage certificate, due to the large size of the district and the number of church registers to be searched (so give details of the church, if known). You can usually search the indexes held locally, for a fee, by making an appointment beforehand.

You should note that the GRO reference you found in the index is of no use to local offices which use a completely different system. Here you will need to quote full details of the event itself: the date and place of birth, marriage or death and the name(s) of the person(s) involved.

Please bear in mind that local register offices may not always be able to respond immediately to requests for certificates, their priority being the registration of current events that will ultimately appear in a future genealogist's family tree.

The system described above is based upon the current situation regarding access to certificates of births, marriages and deaths but new legislation is anticipated within the next five years which may change this procedure.

What the certificates can tell you

It is only by obtaining copy certificates that you can find the full details you need. The information contained in them is as follows:

Example birth certificate (blank). Crown copyright - ONS - reproduced by permission of the controller of HMSO.

- ◆ Birth certificates: date and place of birth, full names of child, names of parents (including mother's maiden name), occupation of father, and particulars of informant. From 1986 the mother's occupation is also included.

◆ Marriage certificates: date and place of marriage, full names and ages of both parties, whether bachelor, spinster or widowed, their occupations and addresses, the names and occupations of both fathers, whether the marriage was by banns or licence, and the names of the officiating person and the witnesses. The age of consent has changed over the years. Up to 1929 the minimum age was twelve for girls and fourteen for boys. In 1929 this changed to sixteen for both parties. 'Full age' was twenty-one and over, up until 1969 when it was lowered to eighteen.

Example marriage certificate (blank). Crown copyright - ONS - reproduced by permission of the controller of HMSO.

◆ Death certificates: date and place of death, full name, sex, age and occupation of the deceased, cause of death and details of the informant. More recently these have also included the date and place of birth, the address of the deceased and the maiden surname where applicable.

Example death certificate (blank). Crown copyright - ONS - reproduced by permission of the controller of HMSO.

Where the same address is given on a marriage certificate for both bride and groom, don't assume this means they were living together – stating that they were living in the same parish removed the need to pay two sets of banns fees. Remember too, that parish register entries for marriages give exactly the same information as marriage certificates, and it may be cheaper and easier to look at parish register marriage entries after 1837 than to purchase the certificates (provided that the ceremony took place in a church!).

Suggested further reading

Annal, D., *Using birth, marriage and death records,*
PRO Pocket Guides to Family History, 2002
Wood, T., *Introduction to civil registration,*
Federation of Family History Societies (FFHS), 1994

Church of England parish registers

Civil registration can take a family historian back to the 1830s but to continue working through the generations you will have to consult the relevant parish registers.

Extract from the first Stevenage parish register showing marriages in 1538 (Ref. DP/105/1/1).

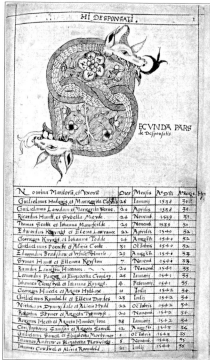

The practice of keeping parish registers began in England and Wales in 1538, when Thomas Cromwell ordered the clergy to keep written records of baptisms, marriages and burials. Many clergymen did not comply, and registers of this date (1538-9) survive for only sixteen of Hertfordshire's 132 ancient parishes. It was not until 1558 that most parishes began to keep registers.

Guidance as to what should be included when recording events was initially minimal, and the usefulness of the early registers to family historians therefore varies considerably. Often entries include only the barest of details, such as the date of the event and the name of the person, but sometimes the information is much fuller, with occupation and place of residence within the parish recorded.

During the Civil War, registers may include dates of birth and death, as well as dates of baptism and burial. In 1653 the Commonwealth government transferred the registration of births and deaths away from the incumbent to the newly-elected 'Parish Register' and at the same time introduced civil marriage. The status quo was restored in 1660 but parish registers of this period may reflect the upheaval of the times.

No standard format was imposed on the registers in England and Wales until 1753 when Hardwicke's Marriage Act attempted to deal with the problem of 'clandestine' and 'irregular' marriages. From 1754 marriage details were required to be kept in a separate volume, with the entry signed by both parties to the marriage and by witnesses. In 1812 Rose's Act introduced separate registers for baptisms and burials too, similarly in volumes of printed forms. From this date baptism entries should contain the names, address and occupation of the parents, and burial entries should contain the age and address of the deceased. The last major change came with the Marriage Act of 1836 when the format of marriage registers was altered to that still in use today. Henceforth, duplicate registers were required to be maintained, one certificate being forwarded to the local superintendent registrar following completion, for inclusion in the civil registration indexes.

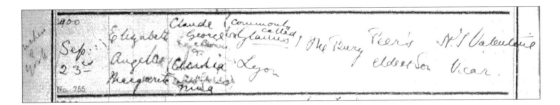

Where to find the records

The registers of nearly all Hertfordshire parishes (other than those currently in use) have been deposited at HALS. A list of those microfilmed for use in the Family History Centre at HALS, dating up to about 1900, is given in Appendix I (including those where original copies are held elsewhere). Films of parish registers are also held at some Hertfordshire libraries (see Appendix V).

It is perhaps not surprising that over the centuries registers may have been lost or damaged. The registers for the parishes of Caldecote, Ickleford and Sacombe, for instance, do not survive before the eighteenth century, and those for the parish churches of Northaw and All Saints' Hertford were badly burned in fires. However, since 1929 the Church of England has taken a keen interest in the survival of its parish registers and has made it mandatory for incumbents to deposit any records over 100 years old in designated Diocesan Record Offices, in which capacity HALS has been recognised since 1932.

Some parish registers that family historians wish to consult may still be with the incumbent concerned, particularly if the parish is a small one and the register has not yet been completed. In this case, parish clergy are entitled to make a charge for consultation, and you should approach the appropriate incumbent by letter in the first instance, giving full details of your request and asking for further information. Some clergy will make the registers available for a personal search, while others will search a limited

Entry from the St Paul's Walden register of 1900 showing the Queen Mother's baptism (Ref. DP/113/1/7).

period for you, but you should be aware that this is entirely at their own discretion.

A number of Hertfordshire parish registers have been transcribed (wholly or in part) and these transcriptions either published or in manuscript can be found at HALS. Many of these are name indexed. A full list is available in the Family History Centre; see Appendix I for an indication of the date coverage for each parish.

Suggested further reading
Gibbens, L., *An introduction to church registers,* FFHS, 1994

Bishops' transcripts
Bishops' transcripts (BTs) are contemporary copies of entries in the parish registers of baptisms, marriages and burials. Family historians may find them invaluable when the original registers have not survived or have been damaged, and in some cases they pre-date the earliest surviving registers.

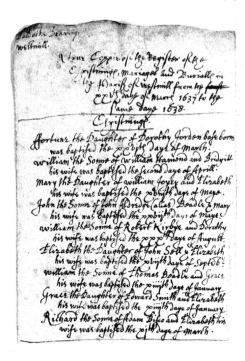

In 1561 the clergy were instructed to send to their bishop each year a transcript of the previous year's entries in parish registers. However, many ignored the order and it had to be repeated in 1597 and again in 1604.

Although these bishops' transcripts are meant to be copies of actual register entries, it is not unknown for BTs to differ in detail from the parish registers. Sometimes entries have been omitted, perhaps because the vicar did not want to highlight the baptism of illegitimate children. Elsewhere, though, entries may have been added that were not in the parish register. As well as filling gaps in coverage, they can therefore be useful aids to checking doubtful dates or spelling and to discovering whether an event has been left out of the register itself. However, Hertfordshire's BTs are also incomplete, with numerous gaps in the series; a common situation with these records. After 1837 returns of marriages were sent to the Registrar General and so they will not normally be included in BTs after that date.

Extract from the bishops transcript of Westmill, 1637/8 (Ref. AHH 15/73)

Where to find the records
All but a few of Hertfordshire's surviving BTs are held at HALS, in the relevant archdeaconry collections. See Appendix I for a list by parish of BTs on microfilm in the Family History Centre.

BTs for parishes within the old Archdeaconry of St Albans (HALS: ASA20) date from the 1560s, with the earliest being from Codicote and St Paul's Walden in 1561, while those from within the Archdeaconry of Huntingdon date from 1604 (HALS: AHH20).

BTs for parishes within the Archdeaconry of Middlesex (Essex and Herts. Division) are held at HALS from 1800 only. The majority of earlier BTs for this part of Hertfordshire have been lost and the few remaining, which cover only the years 1629 or 1630, are held at the Guildhall Library in London. Copies on microfilm are in the Family History Centre at HALS.

BTs are generally available for most parishes in Hertfordshire up to the 1870s, after which time the requirement to make annual returns appears to have lapsed.

Transcripts of the BTs for some parishes, both published and manuscript, are to be found on the shelves in the Family History Centre.

Suggested further reading
Gibson, J., *Bishops' Transcripts and Marriage Licences*, FFHS, 5th ed., 2001

Marriage licences and banns
Church marriages in England and Wales were (and still are) by banns or by licence. From 1754, the fact of whether a marriage has been by banns or licence will be noted in the marriage register and on the marriage certificate after 1837. Both forms generate additional records useful to the family historian and may help to reveal, for instance, a person's place of origin.

Since the thirteenth century, the most common form of church marriage has been by the calling of banns. These are read out on three consecutive Sundays in the church where the marriage is to take place, giving formal notice of a couple's intention to marry. The publication of banns was not often recorded until specifically required by the format of the new marriage registers from 1754 onwards; after 1823 they are contained within a separate banns register.

Extract from the marriage register of Great Gaddesden, 1797 (Ref. DP/39/1/6)

The banns register may give additional information on an individual's place of origin, as from 1823 the banns were required to be called in both parishes of residence, if applicable.

The alternative form of marriage was by licence. Where this was the case there is usually some mention of it in the marriage register. Licences, which were often used for convenience, privacy (there being no need for public banns) or as a status symbol, were obtained from the bishop or archdeacon in whose diocese or archdeaconry the marriage was to be solemnised, on payment of a fee. It was the intention that the licence to marry should apply to the church in one of the spouses' home parishes, but in practice this was often ignored.

In Hertfordshire some copy licences have survived amongst the records of the relevant archdeaconry. It is, however, the 'bonds' and 'allegations' that accompanied the issue of the licence, rather than the licence itself, which are more useful for family historians; the actual licence was usually handed by the couple to the person conducting the marriage ceremony and was rarely preserved. Allegations were sworn statements that there was no legal impediment to the marriage, and could include information such as ages, occupations, marital status and places of residence for the couple, plus the details of a parent or guardian if one or both were under age. Bonds, which were no longer required after 1823, were similarly sworn statements that no impediment existed and that consent had been obtained if either of the couple was under twenty-one; a sum of money had to be pledged as surety that the facts were correct.

In the case of both banns and licences, finding such a record proves only that a marriage was planned, not that a marriage actually took place.

Allegation from a marriage licence concerning John Davies & Mary Freeth, 1801 (Ref AHH20/47).

Where to find the records

Banns books that survive for Hertfordshire (except those in current use) are held at HALS under the parish concerned . They are listed in Appendix I, giving an indication of the years available.

Records of the earliest surviving licences within the archdeaconries of Huntingdon (Hitchin Division) and St Albans appear in the act books of the relevant archdeacon. They have been transcribed from the original

Latin in William Brigg's *Hertfordshire Genealogist and Antiquary,* which is available at HALS: Archdeaconry of St Albans 1583-1715, Archdeaconry of Huntingdon 1610-49. Later licences have been filmed for the Family History Centre and have also been included in the Hertfordshire Marriage Index (see below).

Marriage licences issued within the Archdeaconry of Middlesex (Essex and Herts. Division) are held at the Essex Record Office with the majority of the other records of that archdeaconry.

Where individuals lived in different dioceses, they had to obtain a licence from the appropriate archbishop, and in the case of Hertfordshire couples this would have been the Archbishop of Canterbury. These were known as Vicar-General licences and the records are kept at the Lambeth Palace Library but filmed copies of the allegations 1660-1851 are on microfilm at the Society of Genealogists.

Suggested further reading
Gibson, J., *Bishops' Transcripts and Marriage Licences,* FFHS, 5th ed., 2001

Nonconformist and other non-Anglican records
The term 'nonconformist' embraces all groups which have broken away or dissented from the beliefs and practices of the Church of England since the seventeenth century. Searching for, and identifying, nonconformist ancestors can be a difficult task but most of the surviving registers for Hertfordshire can be consulted at HALS' Family History Centre. This section also offers suggestions for the tracing of Roman Catholic and Jewish ancestors in Hertfordshire.

Henry VIII's Act of Supremacy, passed in 1534, severed the links between England and the Roman Catholic Church and in its place established the Church of England, with the monarch at its head. The restoration of the monarchy in 1660, after the Civil War, saw the Church of England firmly established as the state church. However, this heralded a period of increasing hostility and persecution towards both Roman Catholics (recusants) and those Protestants who chose not to follow the Anglican faith and, under the Act of Uniformity of 1662, the nonconforming clergy were finally ejected from the Church of England. Entries relating to baptisms, marriages and burials of suspected protestant dissenters are likely, therefore, to be found in Anglican parish registers for this early period.

The Toleration Act of 1689 at last allowed nonconformists the right to their own places of worship, teachers and clergy, subject to the swearing of certain oaths of loyalty and declarations. Separate registers of births/baptisms and burials may survive from this date. Searching for entries relating to nonconformist families can be a difficult task and it is very probable that many events were not recorded at all. Also, very few chapels had burial grounds of their own and so Anglican churchyards continued to be used for this purpose until the founding of municipal cemeteries in the nineteenth century.

Although frowned upon as irregular, it was possible to contract a 'common law' marriage in England and Wales by making a declaration before witnesses. In this way Quakers and other nonconformists were able to celebrate marriages in their own meeting houses, but as far as is known only records of Quaker marriages contracted in this way survive for the period before 1754 in Hertfordshire. Hardwicke's Marriage Act of 1753 made such weddings illegal (except for Quakers and Jews) and exacted heavy penalties on those attempting to marry in such fashion, forcing nonconformists to marry in Anglican parish churches. By the terms of the Marriage Act of 1836 nonconformist churches and chapels could be licensed for the solemnisation of marriages upon payment of a fee, which made it unlikely that small congregations ever did this. The establishment of the system of civil registration from 1 July 1837 allowed marriages to take place in a register office. Many nonconformists took advantage of this new system rather than marry in an Anglican church opposed to their religious views.

Extract from a Quaker Digest showing marriages (Ref. NQ1/5C/1).

Book.	Page.	Name.	Residence.	Description.	Names of Parents.
38	233	Pryor Elizabeth			Robert and Elizabeth Pryor
38	235	Phillips Micheal	Royston, Co. of Hertford	Malster	Micheal and Emma Phillips
38	237	Phillips Robert	Royston, Co. of Hertford	Draper	Micheal and Emma Phillips
27	8	Pryor Susanna			William and Sarah Pryor
27	20	Pryor Christopher	Mepsley, in Luton Dist. Beds.	Farmer	John and Ann Pryor
27	24	Pryor Elizabeth	Hertford		William and Elizabeth
38	259	Poole Hannah	Royston, Co. of Hertford	Widow	William and Ann Wicks
2/71	2/5	Pryor Ann			John and Ann Pryor
2/71	382/43	Pain Benjamin	Chesham, in Buckingham	Grocer	Phillip and Elizabeth Pain

The nonconformist groups you are most likely to find within Hertfordshire include:

◆ **The Society of Friends or Quakers:** The Society was founded in the mid-seventeenth century by George Fox, the son of a Leicestershire weaver. Although persecuted during the Commonwealth and excluded from public life, the sect spread rapidly throughout England until the early eighteenth century. It was established in Hertfordshire in about 1655 when Fox visited Hertford, Hitchin and Baldock. The hierarchical administrative structure that developed produced a considerable amount of records. Particularly important, prior to 1837, was the recording of marriages so as to ensure their validity. Quakers recorded births rather than baptisms and, unlike other nonconformists, often had their own burial grounds.

◆ *Baptists:* The Baptist church was founded by separatists within the Church of England in 1611 and by 1633 it had itself split between the Particular Baptists and those that remained as the General Baptists, the former becoming the more numerous body by the end of the century. In 1891 the two groups reunited as the Baptist Union of Great Britain and Ireland. It should be remembered that members of a Baptist church do not practise infant baptism, so that their registers will record births of their members' children and their subsequent baptism as adults.

◆ *Presbyterians, Congregationalists and Independents:* By the late seventeenth century Presbyterians formed the largest nonconformist denomination. By 1850 there were more than 2,000 Congregational chapels in England and Wales. In 1972 the Presbyterian and many of the Congregational churches amalgamated to form the United Reformed Church (distinguished in the table in Appendix II by the reference 'NR').

◆ *Methodists:* The Methodists originally started within the Anglican church in the 1730s but broke away by the end of the eighteenth century under the influence of two ministers, John Wesley and George Whitfield, who wanted to encourage a more lively sense of religion. George Whitfield found a patroness in the Countess of Huntingdon, and chapels following his doctrines were known as *The Countess of Huntingdon's Connexion.* They are now associated with the Congregational Union of England and Wales. The Primitive Methodists emerged as an off-shoot of the Wesleyan Methodists as a result of the evangelical revival of the nineteenth century, and proved popular in the northern and rural areas of the country. In 1932, the two were reunited.

Where to find nonconformist records

The first place to look for nonconformist ancestors, particularly for early events, would be the Anglican parish registers, while post-1837 births, marriages and deaths will be recorded by the Registrar General within the system of civil registration.

With the exception of Quaker registers, not much survives for Hertfordshire prior to the mid-eighteenth century. In 1837 nonconformist congregations nationally were asked to deposit their records with the Registrar-General; not all did so, but those records that were transferred are now held by the Public Record Office at Kew (PRO: RG4).

Microfilm copies of the Hertfordshire registers are available in the Family History Centre at HALS (see Appendix II for a full listing).

Some churches, particularly Congregational, Independent or Baptist, can be known by any of these names at different times, so it is wise to look under each heading until you find a reference to the church in which you are interested. Be aware, too, that nonconformist churches are organised along different lines to those of the Church of England, and are not based on the parish. For example, one register may cover more than one chapel, and an organisational area such as a Methodist Circuit may cover several counties. A chapel may change its denomination or organisational area over time. Some records may therefore be held by neighbouring county archives. Bedfordshire County Record Office, for instance, holds the St Albans Quaker marriage clearances 1676-1779 (BEDS: FR 3/9-10), and more modern Methodist baptism records for Darley Hall chapel, King's Walden (1935-59), Hudnall chapel, Little Gaddesden (1940-85), and Bendish chapel, St Paul's Walden (1939-67).

Transcripts of the registers of Society of Friends' burial grounds have been deposited with HALS as the diocesan registry; see below, *Cemeteries and Crematoria.*

Records may still be held by the chapel. A modern telephone directory will confirm whether it is still in existence. The catalogue of nonconformist records deposited at HALS includes brief histories of many of the chapels, and might indicate where additional records are to be found. Rolls of members or attendance registers are also held for some chapels.

Roman Catholic ancestors and their records

Catholics were completely excluded from the terms of the 1689 Toleration Act and were not allowed to worship freely until the passing of the Catholic Emancipation Act in 1829.

No records from Hertfordshire Catholic churches are held by HALS. Few Catholic registers pre-date 1750. Some have been published by the Catholic Record Society, 114 Mount Street, London WIY 6AA and by Phillimore and Co. Ltd. Most are still held by the churches themselves, the addresses of which can be found in the yearly publication *The Catholic Directory.*

Jewish ancestors and their records

Synagogues are mainly to be found in the south of the county, the result of increasing migration from London since the 1940s.

Since 1837 Jewish births, marriages and deaths will be recorded by civil registration. Jews were not required to deposit pre-1837 registers with the Registrar General and so they will usually have been retained by the synagogue itself. The Jewish Year Book has listed synagogues and Jewish cemeteries since 1896; addresses for Jewish cemeteries at Cheshunt, Waltham Cross and Bushey are given in Appendix III.

No Jewish records are held at HALS and interested family historians are advised to read one of the specialist guides now available on researching Jewish ancestry.

Suggested further reading

Breed, G., *My ancestors were Baptists,* Society of Genealogists (SoG), 3rd ed., 1995

Clifford, D.J.H., *My ancestors were Congregationalists in England and Wales,* SoG, 2nd ed., 1997

Gandy, M., *Tracing Catholic ancestors,* Public Record Office, 2001

Leary, W., *My ancestors were Methodists,* SoG, 3rd ed., 1999

Milligan, E.H. and Thomas, M.J., *My ancestors were Quakers,* SoG, 1999

Ruston, A., *My ancestors were English Presbyterians/Unitarians,* SoG, 1993

Urwick, W., *Nonconformity in Herts,* 1884

Wenzerul, R., *Jewish ancestors? A beginner's guide to Jewish genealogy in Great Britain,* Jewish Genealogical Society of Great Britain, 2000

International Genealogical Index

The International Genealogical Index (IGI) is a worldwide alphabetical surname index of over 200 million (mainly) baptisms and marriages. It is an invaluable first step towards using parish registers for family history research and an aid to identifying where individuals may have originated, although family historians should also be aware of its limitations.

An extract from the IGI (International Genealogical Index, The Church of Jesus Christ of Latter-day Saints).

The IGI has been compiled from a variety of genealogical sources, but primarily (for UK purposes) from microfilm copies of parish registers and bishops' transcripts, by the Church of Jesus Christ of Latter-day Saints (LDS or Mormons). Although it is now widely used by family historians, it was begun in 1969 for theological purposes, being compiled from two main types of entry: those submitted by LDS church members and those transcribed directly from original records (such as parish registers). The latter category is more reliable, it being relatively easy to check the validity of the entry through the original source. LDS church members have often submitted names for 'temple work' to be done without having first found out whether it has been done before, which explains why there are often multiple entries for the same person.

The IGI is an index, and like all indexes it can be extremely useful, but genealogists should be cautious about constructing family trees from the information given, without checking it against original records. It does not cover every parish in England and Wales (nor every parish in

Hertfordshire), some bishops and local clergy having refused the LDS Church permission to film their records, and in some counties there are large gaps in the information available. Because it does not include burials or deaths (except for a very few entries), the only way to check whether a child recorded as baptised did not in fact die as a minor is to look at the parish registers. It is also worth remembering that the spellings of names and the groupings of surnames can be rather idiosyncratic.

Format of the IGI

The UK section of the IGI is arranged by county, with entries listed chronologically within each surname group, giving the forenames and the date and parish of each event. Despite its many inaccuracies, it can often be a shortcut to finding an entry in the parish registers. It lists such information as the names of the parents (if a baptism) or spouse (if a marriage) and the dates and locations of births, baptisms, marriages, and occasionally other events. It also contains LDS' temple ordinance dates.

While the CD-ROM and Internet versions of the IGI provide complete information about the provenance of the entry, users of the microfiche version should be certain to note down the source numbers from the last two columns (the Batch and Serial numbers), once they have found their ancestor's name. These can help you to locate the actual document from which the information was originally extracted. Using this it may be possible to find additional information or identify the person who submitted the entry. See the beginning of the fiche set for an explanation of the codes.

Where to find the IGI

In Hertfordshire, the IGI for the UK and, to varying degrees of completeness, for other countries of the world, is available on microfiche at HALS, and the Hertfordshire Family History Society also has a complete copy. See Appendix V for those Hertfordshire libraries that hold copies on fiche. There have been several issues of the IGI and in general the later the edition, the more names are included. However, because of a change in the way the information was organised, the 1988 edition may contain some names omitted from the 1992 version. The full IGI is available on the Internet on the LDS Church's FamilySearch site <www.familysearch.org>.

Hertfordshire indexes of marriages and deaths/burials

Tracing a family through several generations from one parish to another, which can be difficult and time-consuming, is immensely helped by the use of local indexes. Unexpected branches of a family with an unusual surname, for instance, are found immediately. There are several Hertfordshire indexes already available, and work is ongoing on further indexing projects within the county.

Hertfordshire Marriage Index

The Hertfordshire Marriage Index was originally compiled by Thomas Allen using a similar system to that employed in Boyd's Marriage Index (an index covering several counties, including some parishes in Hertfordshire, a copy of which is held by the Society of Genealogists). The Allen Index includes all known marriages that took place within the county for the period 1538 to July 1837 (when civil registration began). The sources used to compile the index include parish registers, bishops' transcripts, marriage licences and Quaker registers. With an estimated total of over half a million entries, it is an invaluable tool for those tracing Hertfordshire ancestry.

The Allen Index has now been revised, checked and considerably expanded by Brian Gravestock and transferred to a searchable computer database. In an on-going project, this is being extended through 1837 into the census years, typically to 1855 but in some cases to 1880, and out-of-county marriages will be added when known. Searches can be made on a surname basis, or all the marriages in a particular parish can be viewed; it is also possible to search on the names of witnesses to the marriage. Printouts of the results of a search can be made.

The Marriage Index is currently available only at HALS. In addition to the computer database, there is the Allen index itself and typescript copies of the original marriage register transcripts, arranged alphabetically by parish.

Fleet Marriage Index

The Fleet prison in London was notorious in the seventeenth and first half of the eighteenth centuries as a venue for clandestine and irregular marriages, but many 'ordinary' people also took advantage of the ease and speed of a Fleet service and thousands of Hertfordshire men and women made their way there to be married. An index of nearly 7,000 of them was extracted from the registers by Jack Parker; microfilms of the original registers are available at the PRO and the Family Records Centre (PRO: RG7). Parker's index gives the names and status (e.g. spinster, widow) of bride and groom, their place of origin if recorded, the date of the marriage and the man's occupation if shown. *Fleet Marriages of Hertfordshire People to 1754* has been published by the Hertfordshire Family History Society and is available at HALS and in major Hertfordshire libraries in book form.

Hertfordshire Burial Index

Family History Societies throughout England and Wales took part in a project to transcribe and index all known burials for the years 1800 to 1851 in a National Burial Index. Hertfordshire FHS have produced a Hertfordshire Burial Index which gives more information about the original parish entries than the national project, and which currently holds nearly 140,000 names. These have been taken not only from Church of

England parish registers but also include all nonconformist records available, including Quakers. The index is available on CD-ROM in the Family History Centre at HALS, and from the Hertfordshire Family History Society.

Obituaries Index

Many of the local newspapers held at HALS are indexed for articles of Hertfordshire interest and these indexes are available in the library. There is also a separate obituary index. This is an alphabetical index of names taken primarily from obituaries in the newspapers and periodicals held by HALS. They include people from all backgrounds and the index starts approximately at the end of the nineteenth century and continues to the present day. Each entry gives brief details of the deceased and also the reference of the original source so that the enquirer can refer to this for more information.

Indexed parish registers

Many of the transcribed parish registers (manuscript and published) in the Family History Centre at HALS are name indexed. See Appendix I for an indication of the dates and parishes covered.

Monumental inscriptions

Monumental inscriptions (MIs), which include memorials inside churches as well as churchyard gravestones and tombs, are often overlooked as a source by family historians. Many have eroded or disappeared over the centuries but those that remain may provide invaluable extra information on the deceased's age, occupation, abode, relatives or nature of death.

Drawing of a monumental inscription from North Mymms Church (Ref. Oldfield Vol 5).

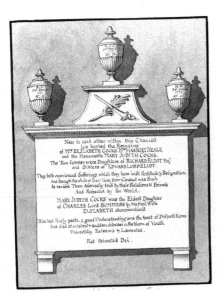

Finding a surviving monumental inscription, usually in the form of a gravestone, will of course depend on the deceased having had a memorial erected to them in the first place. Despite the popularity of memorials during the nineteenth and twentieth centuries, many people were simply too poor or had no surviving family to erect a stone. Even when a memorial is known to have existed, the survival of both the stone and the inscription is unreliable, many having succumbed to Victorian church 'restoration', bomb damage, pollution, vandalism and redevelopment.

Where to find the records

The gravestones or memorials will naturally be found at the parish church but searching for an ancestor's grave can be difficult and frustrating. The most accessible resource for investigating the county's MIs is the ongoing series of lists published since 1982 by the Hertfordshire Family History Society. Most of the county is already covered and the booklets are available in the Family History Centre at HALS. They are usually organised by parish and cover churchyards (not cemeteries), church interiors, other records of names such as war memorials and rolls of honour, and also memorials to the dead which are not necessarily placed on a grave, e.g., a plaque on a tree or seat. Each booklet has a name index and so can be quickly checked, and a sketch map of the location is included. The work is based on an actual survey carried out by volunteers, and checked against older sources, including the Gerish lists noted below.

Some further sources at HALS may also be worth checking, particularly for MIs that may not have survived:

◆ miscellaneous records of MIs may sometimes be found amongst parish records (see the DP catalogues under the parish you are interested in).

◆ copies of some lists made by the local historian W.B. Gerish early in the twentieth century can be found in the Gerish Boxes, alphabetical by parish (HALS: DE/Gr/1-87). Lists compiled by Gerish between 1907 and 1913, which contain 70,000 names, are also in the British Library (BM Add MSS 39271-39284) and at the Society of Genealogists.

◆ a collection of miscellaneous listed or printed MIs is held in the Family History Centre.

◆ nineteenth century county histories (especially those by Clutterbuck and Cussans, see Chapter 9) record the older and more prestigious inscriptions in each parish church.

◆ specialist works on tombs, brasses and epitaphs, such as Rensten, M., *Hertfordshire Brasses: a guide to the figure brasses in the churches of Hertfordshire,* Hertfordshire Publications, 1982, can be found by consulting the catalogues at HALS and major libraries.

Cemeteries and crematoria

The first cemetery, as opposed to church burial ground, in England was opened in 1825 and some of the earliest cemeteries in Hertfordshire date from the mid 1850s. The records can supplement information gained from death certificates on nineteenth and twentieth century ancestors.

Before the middle of the nineteenth century, cemeteries were generally established and run as commercial ventures. Public health concerns were behind the legislation that created municipal cemeteries, as with the rise in population the corresponding overcrowding of churchyards had made many of them, especially in the larger towns, a health risk. An Act of 1850 empowered the General Board of Health, created two years earlier, to establish cemeteries and close urban churchyards, and after that municipal cemeteries became generally accepted as an alternative to burial in the parish churchyard.

An Act of 1852 covering London, and one in 1853 for the rest of the country, established burial boards, and the earliest cemeteries in Hertfordshire were opened in the next few years: Cheshunt, Bishop's Stortford and Hitchin in 1855, Ware in 1857 and Watford in 1858.

The information contained in the registers may vary but can include the name, address, age and occupation of the deceased, the date of death and of burial, and the position of the grave. They are arranged chronologically but are sometimes alphabetically indexed. Cemeteries keep registers of burials, and grave and plot books; cremations were recorded in a separate register. Burial plot deeds also occasionally survive.

Cremation became a legal alternative to burial in 1884 but despite this even by 1947 only one in ten of those who died were cremated. The West Hertfordshire Crematorium was opened in 1959.

Where to find the records

The records of the earlier cemeteries are gradually being deposited with local record offices, but more usually will still be held in the cemetery offices. Deciding which cemetery to search for a particular ancestor's burial can be difficult, as death certificates do not record place of burial. In addition to general municipal cemeteries, there are others devoted to people belonging to particular faiths, such as Catholics and Jews. In Hertfordshire, district councils are responsible for the maintenance of cemeteries, except in East Hertfordshire where the town councils of Bishop's Stortford, Hertford and Ware have that responsibility. Appendix IV lists the cemeteries and crematoria in Hertfordshire, with contact addresses. Please note that some cemeteries do not allow personal searches of the records, although enquiries can be made through the relevant office.

Under the Registration of Burials Act 1864, transcripts of the registers of Society of Friends' (Quakers') burial grounds were required to be deposited in the diocesan registry. The Burials (Beyond the Metropolis) Act 1853 and the Public Health (Interments) Act 1879, dealt similarly with transcripts of other burial grounds and cemeteries. For Hertfordshire, these transcripts are now in the custody of HALS:

◆ Baldock Society of Friends' Burial Ground, 1865 (HALS: DSA 3/3/9)
◆ Bengeo Society of Friends' Burial Ground, 1865-6, 1869, 1871-2, 1875 (HALS: DSA 3/3/1)
◆ Broxbourne, 1867-9, 1870, 1872, 1874 (HALS: DSA 3/3/2)
◆ Cheshunt Burial Ground, 1855-61, 1862-4, 1865-6 (HALS: DSA 3/3/6)
◆ Hertford Cemetery, 1907-20, 1923-47 (HALS: DSA 3/3/7)
◆ Hitchin Cemetery, 1857-68 (HALS: DSA 3/3/8)
◆ Hitchin Society of Friends' Burial Ground, 1865-9, 1871 (HALS: DSA 3/3/3)
◆ Royston Society of Friends' Burial Ground, 1865 (HALS: DSA 3/3/4)
◆ Ware Cemetery, 1865, 1871, 1873 (HALS: DSA 3/3/5)

Some records for prominent London cemeteries where nineteenth-century nonconformists may be buried are held at the PRO.

The following cemetery registers have also been deposited at HALS:

- ◆ Rickmansworth Cemetery, 1857-1961 (HALS: Off Acc 546)
- ◆ St Albans Cemetery, 1884-1918 (HALS: Off Acc 1162, mf)

Coroners' inquests

If an ancestor died an unnatural, sudden or suspicious death, coroners' inquests can occasionally be a source of further information. However, a report of an inquest in the local newspaper will often be the only surviving account, though family historians may discover that this in any case will usually be far more useful to them than the records themselves. All coroners' inquest files and post mortem reports are subject to a statutory closure period of seventy-five years.

A coroner's inquest is a court of law, although before the twentieth century it would often take place in an inn or hotel close to where the body was found, that being the only nearby public building. Until 1926 all inquests were held before a jury who were required to view the body of the deceased. The majority of surviving records will list simply the verdict, the name of the deceased, the date, time, cause and place of death, and the signatures of the jurors; more modern inquests will include medical evidence. Other evidence, such as witness statements, rarely survives. This is often, however, quoted verbatim in newspaper reports. Although all cases of sudden death are reported to the coroner, an inquest is not necessarily held; the coroner will decide whether or not an inquest is necessary, after receiving medical advice.

Until the eighteenth century a single coroner served the whole of Hertfordshire, but by 1796 there were two coroners in the county, one for the Eastern Division and one for the Western. In 1852 four districts were created: Hemel Hempstead, Hertford, Hitchin and St Albans. By 1875 the Hertford Division had been divided into three districts: Bishop's Stortford, Royston and Hertford. Watford was added in 1898. In about 1960 Royston was absorbed into Hitchin Division, and on 1 January 1975 the St Albans and Watford Divisions were combined. An inquest is held by the coroner in whose division the death occurs.

Where to find the records

Before 1752, coroners handed their records over to the assize judges, who deposited them with King's Bench. Any surviving records for this period will be at the PRO (PRO: KB). Medieval coroners' records were deposited with the Court of King's Bench when it visited the county and the rolls and files will also be at the PRO (PRO: JUST). A published source is Cockburn, J.S., *Calendar of Assize Records: Hertfordshire Indictments 1558-1625,* HMSO, 2 vols, 1975. This is available at HALS.

From 1752 to 1860, coroners were required to file their inquest reports at the Quarter Sessions. The published calendars for the Hertfordshire Quarter Sessions list some coroners' records and, although in general these consist only of coroners' accounts, there are some references to name lists for inquests held. The calendars are fully indexed. *St Albans Quarter Sessions Rolls 1784-1820* published by the Hertfordshire Record Society (1991) includes references to individuals. If an inquest resulted in a trial for murder or manslaughter, the papers will be with the assize court records at the Public Record Office (PRO: CRIM).

Unfortunately, coroners' records in the nineteenth and twentieth centuries tend to have a very poor survival rate, mainly because they were in the past generally considered to be part of the personal papers of the coroner concerned. The main covering dates of existing case papers at HALS for the various coroners' divisions are given below. Note that many are closed for seventy-five years: application to see closed files should be made in the first instance, in writing, to the appropriate coroner (a list is available at HALS), but only in exceptional circumstances would they be available to family historians.

- Bishop's Stortford: 1953-8
- Hemel Hempstead: 1908-59 (incomplete), 1988-96 (papers 1960-88 have been destroyed); registers of deaths 1960-92
- Hertford: inquest book 1827-40; inquest papers 1870-83; 1904; 1912; case papers 1934-96
- Hitchin: case papers 1960-96; inquest papers 1972-94; non-inquest papers 1973-92
- St Albans (later St Albans-Watford): case papers 1942-96
- Watford: case papers 1944-74; registers 1964-74

None of these records have been catalogued; for a complete list searchers should consult the *Summary List of Uncatalogued Official Records (Miscellaneous)* at HALS.

Suggested further reading
Cole, J. and Rogers, C., *Coroners' inquest records*,
    Historical Association, 1995
Gibson, J. and Rogers, C., *Coroners' records in England and Wales*,
    FFHS, 2nd ed., 2000

Wills, administrations and inventories
Wills, administrations and inventories are among the most useful sources for family historians, not only for the evidence they provide for family relationships, but also for the insight they can give into everyday life in the past. Thousands of these documents survive, and it is always worth looking to see if an ancestor left a will, no matter what their station in life.

A will is the written expression of how the deceased wanted his or her property divided up after death. It may provide clues not only to wealth and property, but also to family relationships and religious persuasion. All names mentioned in a will should be carefully noted, as they may prove to be previously unknown family members.

When a person died without making a will (intestate), the court granted letters of administration (often abbreviated to 'admin' or 'admon') to a close relative, friend or creditor of the deceased to enable them to deal with the estate. An administration was also granted in cases where the executor(s) named in a will had died or refused to act. Other representatives were then needed to complete the process. Although these documents may contain very little information other than the name of the administrator, they could add something to what you already know by confirming the deceased's name and address, date of death and value of the estate.

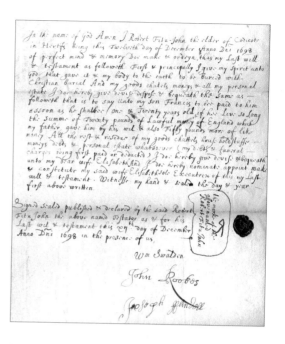

Extract from the will of Robert Fitzjohn of Codicote, 1698 (Ref. 140AW12).

An inventory is a list of the deceased person's moveable goods, made by their representatives. This can provide a fascinating insight into household wealth and personal living conditions, as many list the contents of the house room by room.

Where to find the records before 1858

Before 11 January 1858 when the Principal Probate Registry came into being, wills were proved (registered) in courts administered by the Church. Throughout the country there were about 300 of these courts but most of them had only a very local jurisdiction. In Hertfordshire there were eight ecclesiastical courts with jurisdiction over different parts of the county (see Chapter 1). Not all of the records from these courts are held at HALS and full details are given in Appendix IV, which lists the courts involved and indicates the whereabouts of pre-1858 Hertfordshire wills. (see map, pages 8-9)

The original will signed by the testator was taken to the probate court for registration. This process involved copying the will into a register book. The original wills were then filed at the court, although it is possible that a registered copy may survive where the original has not as the loose documents were more vulnerable. The registered copy is usually much easier to read than the original will written in the testator's own handwriting. Bear in mind also that the majority of wills before 1500 will be written in Latin.

All of the wills kept at HALS, both in original form and registered, have been indexed together. Probate copies of wills made by the court and given to executors can often be found in private collections held by HALS; searchers should consult the personal names index.

The Society of Genealogists also holds a range of relevant indexes: consult Newington-Irving, N., *Will indexes and other probate material in the Library of the Society of Genealogists,* Society of Genealogists, 1996.

Some early wills have been transcribed and published by local societies and individuals:

◆ Munby, L. (ed), *Life and death in Kings Langley: wills and inventories 1498-1659,* Kings Langley Local History and Museum Society: WEA, 1981

◆ Buller, P. and B., *Pots, platters and ploughs: Sarratt wills and inventories 1435-1832,* 1982

◆ Flood, S., *St Albans wills 1471-1500,* Hertfordshire Record Society, 1993

◆ Adams, B., *Lifestyle and culture in Hertford: wills and inventories for the parishes of All Saints and St Andrew 1660-1725,* Hertfordshire Record Society, 1997

◆ Bricket Wood Society, *All my worldly goods: an insight into family life from wills and inventories 1447-1742,* 1991

Inventory of the goods of Richard Stirmon, 1700 (Ref. 137AW14).

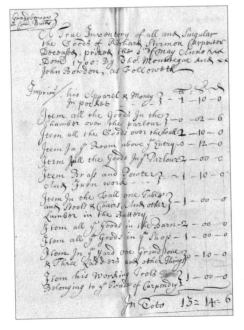

Where a will is proved depends on the location of the property of the deceased person. Hence the importance of knowing the geographical jurisdiction of the individual courts. For example, if a person lived in and owned property in Hertford then the index to the records of the Archdeaconry of Huntingdon (Hitchin Division) should be consulted for a possible will.

If the deceased person had goods worth £5 or more within the jurisdiction of more than one court, but within one diocese, then the will should have been proved in the consistory court of that diocese. If the testator owned property over a much larger geographical area in more than one diocese, then his or her will is more likely to be found amongst the records of the Prerogative Court of Canterbury (PCC). However, it is clear from the records that such rules were not always followed, so if the will cannot be found in the most obvious court then it is advisable to check the records of all the courts where the deceased person may have held property, as well as the PCC. Note also that during the commonwealth period, 1653-60, all wills in England and Wales were proved in the PCC. Published indexes to the PCC wills contain many Hertfordshire entries, which increase in number during the eighteenth century. It became more fashionable for executors to present a will for probate to a court in London, in particular to the PCC, rather than to a small provincial court.

Where to find the records since 1858
From 11 January 1858 the church courts were replaced by a centralised system of civil probate registries. All wills, admons., etc. proved in England and Wales, and British Dependencies, from 1858 to date are held at the Principal Probate Registry, First Avenue House, 42-49 High Holborn, London WC1V 6NP.

Annual indexes (national probate calendars) to all wills registered in the British Isles and dependent territories such as Barbados and South Africa were published from 1858. HALS has these on microfiche for the period 1858 to 1943.

The calendar entry will give you the name of the deceased, his or her occupation (if any), address and date of death, the gross value of the estate, names of executors or administrators and their occupations, addresses and relationship to the deceased (if any).

You can view the actual will or letters of administration at First Avenue House and buy copies; copies can also be ordered by post from the Postal Searches and Copies Department, York Probate Sub-Registry, Duncombe Place, York YO1 7EA.

Suggested further reading
Churchill, E., *Probate jurisdictions: where to look for wills*, FFHS, 5th ed., 2002

Collins, A., *Basic facts about wills after 1858 and First Avenue House*, FFHS, 2001

Gibson, J. and Cox, J., *An introduction to wills, probate and death duty records*, FFHS, 1998

Scott, M., *Prerogative Court of Canterbury wills and other probate records*, PRO, 1997

Adoption and children's homes
Family historians whose relatives were brought up in children's homes, or were adopted, may find it difficult to trace the records that will enable them to build up a family tree. In most cases, information will be available only to the individuals themselves, if at all, and any records containing personal details are closed to inspection for sixty years. This is a complex and sensitive area of research and only a brief account of the background and sources is given below.

Adoption

Adoption did not become legal until the Adoption of Children Act 1926 which came into effect the following January. Before this informal 'adoptions' often took place, sometimes accompanied by a formal agreement or covenant by the parents. Under the Adoption of Children Act 1939, agencies arranging adoption had to be registered by county councils, and Hertfordshire County Council itself acted in this capacity. The only other agency registered in the county was the St Albans Diocesan Adoption Society which operated between 1954 and 1977.

A number of national and other societies registered elsewhere also operated in the county. For information about these and the whereabouts of their records, see Stafford, G., *Where to find adoption records,* British Agencies for Adoption and Fostering, 3rd ed., 2001.

Where to find the records

It will not normally be possible for family historians to trace the origins of adopted persons. Before 1930, however, the various Boards of Guardians were responsible for adoptions and so searching board minutes and other records may prove fruitful (HALS: BG). To do this you will, of course, have to have some idea of the area where the adoption took place.

If the adoption was arranged through one of the national children's societies, contact the relevant body direct.

Anyone who is themselves adopted and intending to search for information is advised to contact Hertfordshire County Council's Children, Schools and Families Department, or one of the organisations set up to help those involved. BAAF (British Agencies for Adoption and Fostering, 11 Southwark Street, London SE1 1RQ), for instance, produces a range of guides and leaflets.

Children's homes

For most of the nineteenth century, babies and children receiving 'indoor relief' were housed in the union workhouse together with all the other categories of pauper. Children may also have been resident in industrial schools, established after 1857 for children in need of care and protection. Towards the end of the century, various unions began to experiment with 'cottage homes' (where children lived and were educated in one place, as at Bishop's Stortford, or Harpenden) and later, 'scattered homes' (the children living in ordinary houses and going to the local school, as at Barnet).

In 1910 unions were instructed that no children over three years old should be housed in the workhouse; they must be placed in cottage or scattered homes, boarded out with foster parents or otherwise cared for. When county councils superseded the boards of guardians in 1930, this situation remained substantially unchanged but, from 1948, when the local children's committees and departments were created (under the

Children's Act 1948), changes began to be made. Moves were made to close the larger and more institutional homes in favour of smaller ones, typified by the four 'family group' homes opened in 1962 in Hemel Hempstead. From 1970 (following the Children and Young Persons Act 1969), the homes were known as 'community homes'.

Where to find the records

Some records of children's homes are held at HALS (HALS: HSS8). These may include registers of admission and discharge, correspondence, etc. In order to preserve confidentiality, the following records will not normally be produced for inspection by general researchers:

- ◆ records containing entries less than sixty years old which contain personal details concerning individuals, including log books of children's homes
- ◆ all other unpublished records containing entries less than thirty years old.

Not all children's homes were run by Hertfordshire County Council; trade directories are useful sources of information before 1937.

Chapter 3

Household and property records

Perhaps the best known household records are the census returns, completed every ten years since 1801. It will be to these that the family historian will turn first, to establish family relationships and discover where their ancestors lived and originally came from. There are other records too, although they do not cover the whole population as the census does, that will give information about individuals and where they lived, such as local population lists, manorial records, parish rate assessments, electoral registers and poll books, and tax returns. In the case of taxes and manorial records, the information is particularly valuable when it pre-dates parish registers and takes the researcher back to medieval times.

Census returns

The national census is particularly important for family historians because, unlike other sources, it not only gives information about individuals but also about family groups and households. It can establish relationships and occupations, identify siblings and other family members and provide the essential link to finding out where your ancestor was originally from.

The first complete census of the population of England and Wales was taken in 1801. Until 1837 the compilation and return of statistics was the responsibility of the parish officers. Those rare records that have survived from this period have done so because they were kept with other parish documents. The 1801 to 1831 returns were concerned only with the number of people, inhabited and uninhabited houses and some occupations, and so do not contain the kind of information available from 1841 onwards.

With the establishment in 1837 of civil registration, the task of compiling the census returns passed to the superintendent registrars. The General Register Office (GRO), now the Office for National Statistics (ONS), retains the records until they are due for public release (after 100 years) and then passes them to the Public Record Office (PRO) to be made available. This means that the last census currently available to view is 1901.

Each census is a 'snapshot' of the population on one particular day, as follows:

1841 – Sunday 6 June	1881 – Sunday 3 April
1851 – Sunday 30 March	1891 – Sunday 5 April
1861 – Sunday 7 April	1901 – Sunday 31 March
1871 – Sunday 2 April	

The superintendent registrars were in overall control of a number of registrars, whose areas were in turn divided into enumeration districts. These were supposed to have been based on existing 'meaningful entities' such as parishes or towns, and were meant to be of a size that an enumerator could travel around in one evening. This equated to about 200 dwellings, which could be just part of a town but might be a rural area of up to thirteen miles, taking in several hamlets. However, in practice the districts varied in size considerably.

The 'census returns' are the compilation forms, statistics and declaration completed by the enumerator. These were compiled from the forms that he delivered to every householder and collected in person, subsequently transcribing them into the census enumerators' books (CEBs). The forms were supposed to be filled in by the head of the household. In practice, the enumerator often had to complete forms for those who could not do it themselves and this has implications for their accuracy. Enumerators did not always spell names, occupations and places correctly, and regional accents could cause further problems. Details could also have been wrongly transcribed from the form to the CEB, and the householders' forms no longer survive for checking against. Enumerators' handwriting can be wonderful Victorian copperplate that is a pleasure to read or an unintelligible scrawl.

Extract from a census page showing residents in Braughing in 1891 (Ref. RG12 1099 ED3 F31).

Where to find the records

Summaries of the statistical information for each parish in England and Wales have survived for all the census years and have been published; they are available for Hertfordshire in the library at HALS. The enumerators' returns for 1801-31, however, with a few rare exceptions have not survived.

In Hertfordshire there are returns for 1801 for Barkway and Reed (HALS: DP/13/3/4) and Hitchin (HALS: 67580).

A complete set of the census returns for Hertfordshire from 1841 to 1901 can be seen at HALS. Main libraries in the county also hold some film of the census returns for their local area (see Appendix V).

The full national census returns are held at the Family Records Centre in London, with computer access to the 1901 census. The PRO has also placed the 1901 census, with a free searchable name index, on the Internet (<www.census.pro.gov.uk>), where it can be viewed for a fee. It is expected that further census years will be published on the Internet in the future.

The 1881 national census has been name-indexed and the fully transcribed returns made available on CD-ROM by the Church of Latter-day Saints (and also on their website <www.familysearch.org>). This can be used at HALS; the Hertfordshire Family History Society and some Hertfordshire libraries (see Appendix V) also hold copies. Surname indexes for the 1851 census for Hertfordshire, compiled by the University of Hertfordshire's Centre for Regional and Local History, are held at HALS, as are those for a substantial portion of the 1891 census (still in progress). The University of Hertfordshire Press has published two volumes (covering the superintendent registrar's districts of Berkhamsted and St Albans) in an on-going series on *Population, economy and family structure in Hertfordshire in 1851,* by Professor Nigel Goose, which include transcriptions of the census returns for those areas, with a name index.

Using the census at HALS

The original documents are organised by PRO 'piece number' as follows (HO stands for Home Office; RG for Registrar General): 1841 – HO 107; 1851 – HO 107; 1861 – RG 9; 1871 – RG 10; 1881 – RG 11; 1891 – RG 12; 1901 – RG 13.

These numbers are followed by enumeration district (ED) numbers and folio (F) numbers. To find the full reference for the place you are seeking, refer to the census place index in the Family History Centre. This gives the full PRO piece number for each place, together with the reel number (in red) of the microfilm on which it appears.

On the microfilm the PRO piece number appears adjacent to each page of the returns, the enumeration district is referred to at the beginning of the relevant section, and the folio numbers are the big, bold numbers stamped on every other page (originally the facing pages). This arrangement is fairly straightforward for returns 1851 onwards. However, the 1841 returns do not follow a logical order and you will need to refer to the census guides (in binders) which detail the streets and areas covered by each enumeration district. These are also located in the Family History Centre.

A summary of the details shown on the returns is as follows:

◆ 1841 – full name, age (up to fifteen years, the age given exactly; over fifteen years, rounded down to the nearest five years), sex, occupation, born in this county (yes or no). The end of each household is shown by one oblique stroke /; end of a building by two oblique strokes //. Relationships between people are not recorded.

◆ from 1851 – full name, relationship to head of household, marital status, sex, exact age, occupation, parish and county of birth, and certain disabilities.

House numbers are not normally shown until the 1881 census, and then only for streets in larger towns like Watford and St Albans. The number shown in the left-hand column of the form is a running schedule number and does not relate to the address of the house.

Suggested further reading

Higgs, E., *A clearer sense of the census*, HMSO, 1996
Lumas, S., *Making use of the census*, PRO Publications, 4th ed., 2001
Using census returns, PRO Pocket Guides, 2000

Electoral registers and poll books

Electoral registers are among the easiest of genealogical sources to use, helping to locate individuals and establish how long families stayed at particular addresses. Poll books pre-date electoral registers and, although they do not cover a great portion of the population, can provide information going back to the seventeenth century.

Electoral registers

The registers are annual lists of persons entitled to vote at elections. They were first published in 1832 and appeared annually (and twice a year between 1919-26 and 1945-9), except between 1916-17 and 1940-4 when none were published because of the wartime emergency.

Extract from an electoral register of 1842 (Ref. QPE/211).

Parish or Hamlet.	No.	Names of Voters.	Place of Abode.	Nature of Qualification.	Street, Lane, or other Place where the Property is situate, or name of the Tenant.
Bushey					
	2939	Sears Samuel	Bushey	Copyhold House	The Mead
	2940	Sims David	Bushey	Copyhold Houses	Bushey Village
	2941	Simmons Henry	Bushey	Occupier of a House & Land at £80 per annum	Bushey Village
	2942	Sharp Edmond Pell	Clay Hill	Copyhold House	Clay Hill
	2943	Smith Bailey	Watford	Freehold Cottages	Bushey Mill Lane
	2944	Stapleton George	Bushey	Two Copyhold Cottages	Bushey Village

The whole of Hertfordshire was contained in a single annual volume until 1895, when the county was divided into parliamentary divisions.

Beginning with just four in 1895 (Eastern or Hertford Division, Northern or Hitchin Division, Mid or St Albans Division and Western or Watford Division), the number of divisions has gradually risen to ten in the current edition. The boundaries of these divisions have also been subject to change and parishes have sometimes moved from one division to another.

Until 1915 the registers are alphabetical by surname. Thereafter they are arranged alphabetically by street name in each polling district. Before 1918 the registers show the name, address and qualifying property owned or leased by the voter. After 1918 just the name and address is given.

The registers were always published several months after the qualifying date and some of the voters may have moved or died by the time the registers were published.

The most important thing to know is who was entitled to vote in any given year. Very briefly, before 1832 only men over twenty-one with freehold land or tenements with an annual net value of 40 shillings or more could vote in county elections, while the borough franchise varied and could include a large proportion of the male population. After 1832 the franchise gradually increased, taking in some new classes of tenant voters in 1832, part of the urban working class in 1867, and rural labourers in 1884. In 1918 the electorate was enlarged to take in men aged twenty-one and over who had lived in a constituency for over six months, and members of the armed forces aged nineteen and over were enfranchised.

Some women were given the municipal vote in 1869 by the Municipal Corporations Act but it was not until 1918 that the majority of women aged thirty and over could vote in parliamentary elections. In 1928, men and women aged twenty-one and over were given equal voting rights. The voting age was lowered to eighteen in 1969.

There were numerous people who were not eligible to vote in parliamentary elections, including lunatics, criminals serving a prison sentence, peers of the realm, non-naturalised foreigners and anyone convicted of election bribery (five-year ban). Until 1918 serving policemen, tax collectors, election officers and agents, customs and excisemen, postmasters and people in receipt of poor relief were excluded, as were World War I conscientious objectors in the 1918 and 1923 elections.

The details of exactly who qualified for the vote at different times can be complicated; *Electoral registers since 1832* contains a useful brief description (see *Suggested further reading*).

Where to find the records

HALS holds electoral registers covering almost the whole period from 1832 and the relevant copy can easily be found by consulting the full list available.

These include:

1832-1915	whole county (some gaps covered by draft electoral registers, see below), except for Hertford Division 1897, 1908, 1914; St Albans Division 1900, 1906
1918-30	whole county except for Hertford Division 1927, 1929, 1930; Watford Division 1927; Hitchin Division 1929
1931	Letchworth and Stevenage only
1932	whole county except for Hertford Division
1933	parishes of Aldbury, Bourne End, Little Gaddesden, Long Marston, Nettleden, Northchurch, Wiggington, Letchworth only
1934	St Albans Division only
1935	Letchworth only
1936	Aldbury, Great Berkhamsted, Little Gaddesden, Nettleden, Potten End, Tring, Chipperfield, Chipping Barnet, Kings Langley, Letchworth only
1937	Letchworth only
1938	Berkhamsted, Hemel Hempstead, Letchworth (draft), Tring Urban only
1939	East Barnet, Chipperfield, Hemel Hempstead Rural, Hoddesdon, Letchworth (draft), Tring Urban, Kings Langley, and Watford Division only
1945	Welwyn Garden City only
1946-7	Letchworth, Tring Urban only
1948-50	Tring Urban only
1951 to date	whole of county (except 1973: part of county)

There are also numerous electoral registers for the Borough of Hertford 1832-1973, and the Borough of St Albans for 1934 (HALS: Off Acc 1162, no. 1849). Registers for the Borough of Watford from 1933 to the present are held at Watford Library.

When a register is not available at HALS (e.g. for the period 1947-50), a copy can be found at the British Library. Hertfordshire libraries hold current electoral registers.

Electoral registers were compiled from amended draft registers. Changes were made to the draft registers resulting from various factors including changes of voters' addresses and deaths of voters. HALS holds draft electoral registers for 1832-89 for the complete county and 1892-3 for part of the county (HALS: QPED/1-136).

Absent voters' registers

An invaluable source for locating military ancestors is the absent voters' register. In 1918 the 'Representation of the People' Act made provision for members of the armed forces, British Red Cross, St John Ambulance

Brigade and anyone whose work was officially recognised as being of national importance to the war, to obtain a vote by post or proxy in their home constituency.

Civilian residence in Hertfordshire was by no means indicative of membership of a Hertfordshire regiment. A survey of 5,000 absent voters across the county showed this accounted for just over three per cent of Hertfordshire's serving soldiers.

The following example shows the type of information contained in an entry:
St Albans

| 1578 | Smith, John Francis | 6 London Road | L/8350 Officers' Steward HMS 'Platypus', RN |

Absent voters' registers were first published in autumn 1918 and then twice yearly between 1919 and 1926 and annually between 1927 and 1931. HALS holds the complete series with the exception of Hitchin in 1923 and St Albans in autumn 1923.

Poll books

Page from a poll book for Edwinstree Hundred, 1727 (Ref. QPE/13).

Before electoral registers came into use, poll books provided a record of electoral information. The difference between the two is that electoral registers show only who was entitled to vote, while poll books also show who they actually voted for.

From 1696 sheriffs were made responsible for recording the poll at parliamentary elections and making the results public. Poll books were therefore kept, and many were commercially published after the election. They continued in use until after the 1868 general election (and so overlap with electoral registers for thirty years), but the introduction of the secret ballot in 1872 put an end to their use. The information contained in them varies considerably. The names of the voters, their place of residence and who they voted for are always listed. Sometimes the voters' addresses, occupations and property qualification to vote are also included. The manuscript books may contain comments about the voter and why he voted as he did (e.g. 'bribed').

Where to find the records

Numerous manuscript and published poll books for elections between 1697 and 1868 are held at HALS; many have been microfilmed. Consult the list available for the full catalogue reference.

```
EDWINSTRY HUNDRED. 9
Richard Manfell      Coddicot                S     C
Edward Brown A.                               F
Edward Currant                                F
Nathaniel Kimpton                             F
Jeremiah Rayment                              F   C
James Pitty       Chifoull, Effex                C
Ralph Flitton   Bafingbourn, Cambridgefhire      C
Richard Mills   London                           C
Thomas Grey                                      C

              Berden.
Benjamin Bocock, Whitechappel              S   F

              Barley.
Thomas Savile                              S   F
Francis Patten                             S   F
John Savile                                S   F
John Potten                                S   F
Richard Searle                             S   F
Nathaniel King                             S   F
William Hannel                             S   F
Thomas Bifcoe                              S   F
Francis Bell                               S   F
William Johns                                  C
William Cakebread                              C
James Hoye                                     C
John Trigg      Elmden, Effex                  C
Robert King     London                         C
Andrew Wolfe    Berkway                        C
John Nicholas   Chifwick, Middlefex.           C

              Buckland.
William Godfrey    Chipping               S   F
Thomas Rumbald     Royfton                S   F
John Thorn      Barley                    S   F
Robert Auftin                             S   F
John Cock                                 S   F
Matthew Clayton                           S   F
William Bray                              S   F
```

- County elections – manuscript poll books: 1697, 1708, 1714, 1722, 1727, 1734, 1736, 1754, 1761, 1774, 1790, 1796, 1802, 1803
- County elections – published poll books: 1722, 1727, 1734, 1754, 1774, 1784, 1790, 1796, 1805, 1832, 1852 (Hertford polling district only)
- Hertford Borough elections – manuscript poll books: 1727
- Hertford Borough elections – published poll books: 1831, 1837, 1868
- St Albans Borough elections – manuscript poll books: 1715, 1780, 1802, 1812, 1818
- St Albans Borough elections – published poll books: 1820, 1821, 1830, 1832, 1835, 1847

Suggested further reading
Gibson, J., and Rogers, C., *Poll books c1696-1872: a directory to holdings in Great Britain,* FFHS, 4th ed., 2002
Gibson, J., and Rogers, C., *Electoral registers since 1832; and burgess rolls,* FFHS, 2002

Tax returns
Tax returns, with their listings of names and details of liability, are an unusual but useful source for genealogists. Some date from medieval times when records may be scarce or unavailable.

Lay subsidies
From the twelfth century to the seventeenth century, lay people (i.e. non-clergy) were regularly taxed on moveable property (e.g. goods or wages). These taxes are known as lay subsidies, recorded on subsidy rolls.

Medieval lay subsidy returns mentioning individuals exist among the records of the Exchequer only up to 1334. Up to then a number of subsidies had been levied, ranging from a fifth to a twentieth of moveable wealth. In 1334 fixed quotas were set for each shire and thereafter the Exchequer was not concerned with the actual people who were paying the tax. It was not until the early sixteenth century following Henry VIII's alterations to the tax system that listings of individuals returned. Those for 1524 and 1525 are particularly comprehensive.

These early returns are held by the Public Record Office (PRO: E179) and are in county and date order. Single or widowed women are included as well as men. Microfilm copies of the PRO subsidy rolls (PRO: E179/120/5, 8, 10) are held at HALS for 1294/5, 1307/8 and 1314/15 (HALS: PC 782).

Some Hertfordshire returns (1568-1603) are also available at HALS (HALS: Acc 3116). A transcript of the Hertfordshire subsidy rolls (1290/1) is catalogued under the reference DE/Sa/11.

There are transcripts of the subsidy rolls for Hertfordshire in 1545 and 1566/7 (Dacorum Hundred only) in Brigg, W., *Hertfordshire Genealogist and*

Antiquary. A transcription of the 1307 and 1334 subsidy rolls appears in Brooker, J., and Flood, S., *Hertfordshire Lay Subsidy Rolls 1307/8 and 1334,* Hertfordshire Record Society, 1998.

Poll taxes

Poll taxes were levied on each head of population and therefore affected far more people than the lay subsidies. It was the poll tax of one shilling per head that provoked the Peasants' Revolt in 1381.

The returns for the poll taxes of 1377, 1379 and 1381, as well as those for the seventeenth century (1641-98), are held by the Public Record Office (PRO: E179).

Hearth tax

Introduced from 25 March 1662, this was a tax on householders of two shillings on each fire hearth or stove in every dwelling place in their occupation, payable annually in two instalments at Lady Day (25 March) and Michaelmas (29 September). The tax was abolished in 1688, the last collection date being 25 March 1689.

The returns are an extremely useful source for genealogists because they place individuals in parishes in a certain period. However, this usefulness is somewhat offset by the great number of omissions from the lists, including those too poor to pay poor/church rates, those who occupied premises worth less than twenty shillings a year and those who owned property worth less than £10. Occasionally the poor are included at the end of lists but more usually they were left out altogether.

Lists of householders and numbers of hearths were delivered by petty constables to the Justices of the Peace in Quarter Sessions, who certified them and passed them on to the Clerk of the Peace, who in turn had to send a copy on to the Exchequer. No Hertfordshire returns are preserved in the records of the Clerk of the Peace, but copies of those that were sent to the Exchequer and are now held at the PRO (PRO: E179) are available at HALS on microfilm in the Family History Centre (see Appendix I).

The returns dated Lady Day and Michaelmas 1663 are the most complete. Those for Little Amwell, Bishop's Stortford and Ware dated Lady Day 1666 list 'those dead of the plague' or 'dead of the sickness'. No lists appear to survive at all for Bramfield. Some returns from 1662 and 1673 are badly damaged and the film may be difficult to read.

There is an ongoing project by the British Record Society to transcribe hearth tax records; published books so far include Kent, Cambridgeshire and Norfolk.

Window and house tax

This tax was first imposed in 1696 and abolished in 1851. Each householder was taxed two shillings a year, with an additional payment of eight shillings for houses with eight windows or more. Like the hearth tax, the poor were exempt and from 1825 occupiers with fewer than eight windows were also exempt. The surviving returns for Hertfordshire are few:

◆ parish assessments (1712-35) comprising Broxbourne 1712-3; Broadwater Hundred 1715-6,1724-5, 1730,1733,1735 (HALS: LT MISC.10)

◆ duplicates for hundreds (1721-36) showing total amounts levied for parishes in the following hundreds: Braughing 1721, 1729, 1731; Broadwater 1721, 1730, 1733,1735-6; Edwinstree 1721, 1731; Hertford 1721, 1729, 1731 (HALS: LT MISC.10)

◆ miscellaneous papers 1733-83 (HALS: LT MISC. 8,10)

Land tax

This tax on land valued at more than twenty shillings per annum was regularly imposed from 1692 with the rate varying from four shillings to one shilling in the pound. From 1798 it was made a perpetual tax, but owners were then allowed to change the method of payment by 'redemption', which involved paying a one-off lump sum to the tax commissioners.

Many of the Hertfordshire returns date from the early 1700s. The earliest is for Northchurch in 1705, though others start in 1711. The returns for some parishes, however, do not start until as late as 1798.

Example of land tax records for Cheshunt, 1789 (Ref. QS records).

From 1780 to 1832, payment of the tax was evidence of eligibility to vote in elections and copies of the returns were kept by the Clerk of the Peace; after 1832 this was no longer the case and so most surviving Hertfordshire returns date only to about this time. There was a second period when returns for some parishes were kept, however, from 1863 to 1891.

The returns are available in the Family History Centre at HALS on microfilm (see Appendix I for coverage by parish). They give the name

and amount of assessment for each person taxed. After 1798 the sums assessed are shown in two columns: 'exonerated' or 'not exonerated', referring to the method of redemption mentioned above. The names of both owners and occupiers are given on the later forms.

Tithes and tithe maps

The obligation to pay one tenth of all produce to the church, known as 'tithe', had existed from early times and was made compulsory in the tenth century. The system was complex and disputes often arose over the assessment and subsequent collection of the tax, which was paid 'in kind' and involved the handing over of a part of the annual crop or every tenth animal. Many landowners eventually reached agreements with their parish clergy to change the tithe due into a simple cash payment.

Extract from the tithe map of Ashwell, 1841 (Ref. DSA4/6/2).

The Tithe Act of 1836 set up a body of commissioners to supervise the changeover into a cash sum of all remaining payments in kind. In order to fix a fair assessment of the exact money owed for each piece of property, a survey was undertaken. This resulted in the drawing up of a large-scale plan of each parish affected, together with a schedule, known as the tithe award and apportionment. Three copies were made – one for the parish clergyman, one for the diocesan registrar and a third for the Tithe Commissioners. The first two of these copies for Hertfordshire are now held at HALS (HALS: DP or DSA 4). The third will be amongst the records of the Tithe Commissioners at the Public Record Office (PRO: IR).

HALS holds tithe maps for 120 Hertfordshire parishes dating from 1838 to 1851. Where no original is available, a microfilm copy is kept (e.g., Harpenden, Offley, East and Chipping Barnet, Buckland, Shephall, Ware). Although not all of these are detailed, the coverage is remarkably complete for a shire county. In those parishes for which no tithe survey was made, it will usually be found that there had been an enclosure survey and award a few years before.

For many Hertfordshire villages the tithe survey is often the first large-scale map on which individual buildings can be clearly identified, predating the first edition of the Ordnance Survey map, not published for Hertfordshire until 1878. Many buildings are coloured – red for dwellings, grey for others. Plot numbers on the maps correspond to those on the schedules, which list owners and occupiers of properties, together with the amount of tithe payable. Surveys, which predate the first detailed census of 1841, can provide family historians with vital evidence for the place of residence and property ownership of their ancestors.

Inland Revenue records (1910)

Following the Finance Act 1910, land was surveyed for valuation by the Commissioners of Inland Revenue for a proposed tax. The resulting records (HALS: IR) are coloured-up maps based on the second edition Ordnance Survey maps of the county, with accompanying valuation books (or 'domesday books') which record information on owners, occupiers and their property. These documents are actually the working copies of the survey, the final copies (field books and plans) being held by the Public Record Office (PRO: IR58).

Parish rate assessments

Rate assessments may be able to confirm the whereabouts of an ancestor at a given date, particularly useful because they pre-date directories and the census.

The Poor Law Relief Act of 1601 empowered overseers of the poor in each parish to levy compulsory rates on the occupiers of property in order to help pay for the cost of relieving the poor. From the seventeenth century onwards, different types of rate financed the various other local responsibilities of the parish. For example, parish churchwardens collected a church rate (until 1868) in order to maintain the church and churchyard, and highway rates were also raised by the surveyor of the highways.

Following the Local Government Act of 1894, the new district councils became responsible for collecting rates, although the office of overseer of the poor was not abolished until 1925. The Rating and Valuation Act of 1925 reformed the rating system and introduced the general rate in place of the old parish rates.

From a rate assessment of Abbey Parish, St Albans, 1724 (Ref. DP/90/11/1).

Early parish rate assessments may be found as separate sheets but quite often they were bound up with the overseers' accounts. From the late eighteenth century, books printed with columns and headings began to be used. Occupiers of property were responsible for paying rates and the earlier parish rate books often merely list the occupiers and the amount of rate paid.

In order to help the collectors locate properties, assessments were either divided into areas of the parish, or properties were listed street by street, giving house numbers (if numbering had come into use). Sometimes a brief description is given of a property. After the 1834 Poor Law Amendment Act it became more common for both the owners and occupiers of the property to be given. Following the Rating and Valuation Act of 1925, information found in rate books includes the name of the occupier and owner and a description of the property.

How much ratepayers would be asked to pay was determined by the rateable value of their property, as shown by the valuation list. The compilation of valuation lists was the duty of local authorities until 1948, when the valuation officers of the Commissioners of the Inland Revenue took over this responsibility.

Where to find the records

A number of Hertfordshire parishes have surviving rate assessments from the seventeenth century but, in general, they are found only from the eighteenth and nineteenth centuries. Few parishes have a continuous series and gaps are common. The assessments are held with the parish records (HALS: DP).

Rate books of the twentieth century survive in greater numbers and from the 1950s are more likely to exist in a continuous series. Rate books and valuation lists are held within the district council records (HALS: UDC/RDC).

Manorial records

Ancestors who held copyhold property may well be named within manorial records. Although of medieval origin, some manorial courts were still being held into the twentieth century, and it may also be possible to identify ancestors who were brought before the court for a misdemeanor or to settle a local quarrel.

Extract from a court roll of the manor of Great Tring, dated 23 October 1677, showing the transfer of lands of Lawrence Washington, lately deceased (great uncle of George Washington) to Richard Jones on behalf of Mary Washington, aged 13, heir of Lawrence (Ref. DE/Vy/M9).

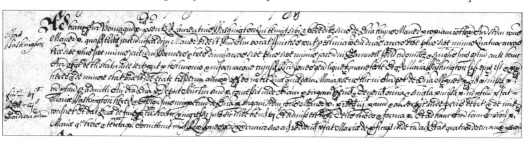

The origins of the manor are uncertain but by the time of Domesday Book in 1086 the manorial system was established throughout most of England. Today we think of a manor as a large house owned by a fairly well-to-do country gentleman, but in medieval times a manor meant a single administrative unit of a landed estate, which may or may not have included a dwelling house for its lord.

By the fifteenth century the manor had become defined in law as a piece of landed property with tenants over whom the lord exercised certain rights in his private court. This manorial court was usually held every three weeks. The lord used the court to enforce the payment of all dues and the performance of all services owed to him by his tenants. Some courts had powers to settle local disputes (so that names of complainant and defendant will appear) and appoint officials such as the constable. In principal all tenants were obliged to attend the court and were fined if they did not. A list of all who attended and those 'in mercy' (i.e. absent) can be found at the beginning of the record of each court – useful evidence for family historians as to the existence of a family surname in the area covered by a manor.

The records of the manorial court become fuller and more formalised in the later medieval period and mainly consist of the transfer of tenants' property from one person to another. A tenant's right to hold his property was written on the manor court rolls, of which he had a copy – hence the term 'copyhold'. All conveyances of copyhold land had to be sanctioned by the manorial lord and the court ensured that his financial interests were preserved. The new tenant would have to pay an entry fee to the lord and whenever a tenant died his heir had to provide a 'heriot' or tribute – the best of the animals, or more usually a substantial money payment.

It is these records, with their details of family relationships, which family historians may find most useful. However, very early court records are written in Latin (until 1733) and you will need to be confident in your reading of period handwriting. They can be very rewarding for those who take the time to understand the old phrases used in the workings of the courts.

Eighteenth and nineteenth century manorial court records are sometimes indexed by name, especially if the steward has copied them into books. At this period the court tended to meet much less frequently so a long gap in a series of court records need not mean that any have been lost. Manorial courts were gradually declining as lords transformed their holdings into freehold tenure. Copyhold was finally abolished under the Law of Property Act of 1922.

Where to find the records

Hertfordshire manorial records held at HALS have been listed alphabetically by the name of the manor. Records may be held in more than one archive, or outside the county, depending on who owned the manor. *The Victoria County History,* or other county histories (see Chapter 9 on Printed Sources) will help you to identify the appropriate lord of the manor.

Finding manorial records in general is not always straightforward, as many, if surviving, may still be in private hands. Following the 1922 Act, efforts were made to protect and preserve such records by encouraging owners to register them on the Manorial Documents Register. This can be consulted at the Royal Commission on Historical Manuscripts (amalgamated with the Public Record Office in April 2003 to form the National Archives; see Appendix VI).

Transcriptions appear in Brigg, W., *Hertfordshire Genealogist and Antiquary* of the Court Rolls of the Manor of Picotts in Bishop's Stortford 1396-1760 (various years, not continuous); Tring Manor 1615-22; Much Hadham 1529; Sandridge 1526; Redbourn 1621-2 and the Rental of the Manor of Hemel Hempstead 1676. See also Howlett, B., *Survey of the Royal Manor of Hitchin 1676,* Hertfordshire Record Society, 2000.

Suggested further reading
Ellis, M., *Using manorial records,* PRO Publications, 1994
Park, P.B., *My ancestors were manorial tenants,* Society of
    Genealogists, 1994

Local population lists
Lists sometimes survive of the residents of part of a town or a village, drawn up for some local purpose, which may be of great interest to family historians.

Lists of the local population were usually made on a parish basis and for a particular purpose. They might be related to the working of the poor law, or to religion, or the vaccination of local children, or perhaps were made simply because the local incumbent was keen on keeping records of his flock. They may note all, or only a proportion, of the inhabitants.

Where to find the records
It is worth looking to see if there are any surviving lists for the parishes you are researching (HALS: DP catalogues). The lists are often to be found within other documents, e.g. vestry minutes, or in a vicar's notebook, and may not be separately catalogued, although a description of them will appear. Not all have been noted here, as they differ in comprehensiveness and usefulness to the family historian, but examples include:

◆ a list of the local inhabitants drawn up by the incumbent of
   Northchurch in 1770 in a survey of the parish (HALS: DP/74/3/3)
◆ besides the list of parishioners in 1801 (drawn up for the census), a
   further list for 1803 included in the incumbent's notes for Barkway
   and Reed (HALS: DP/13/29/4)
◆ an index of children vaccinated in the parish of Aldbury between 1814
   and 1819 (HALS: DP/2/18/2)

♦ for reasons of tithes, a note of the inhabitants of Kimpton in 1700, 1714 and 1718 (HALS: DP/61/1/1), these lists appearing in the middle of the parish register.

Note, too, that the militia ballot lists of the second half of the eighteenth century (see Chapter 8) are effectively a local census of all adult men between certain ages.

Chapter 4

Professions and occupations

Finding out about an ancestor's profession or occupation can give family historians an insight into their day-to-day lives. Census returns, birth, marriage and death certificates, parish records and wills may all record an individual's occupation. How much additional personal information can be obtained from archives may be limited, but there is a wealth of supporting evidence available in, for instance, local history books and museums. This chapter looks at those occupations which in the past had to be licensed, leaving records in Quarter Sessions papers, and others for which archive material may be found. Trade directories (see Chapter 9) will also be helpful in pinpointing where and when certain occupations and industries were active. Records relating to service in the militia or regular army are covered in Chapter 8, Military Ancestors.

Licensed occupations

From medieval times, a licence was required from the authorities, either ecclesiastical or civil, in order to undertake certain occupations. The surviving licences, and the registers kept of those issued, will be useful to family historians as confirmation of an ancestor's occupation in a period when other sources may be lacking.

Victuallers

From 1552 anyone keeping an inn or alehouse had to apply to the Justices of the Peace (JPs) for permission to do so. Landlords were required to give a guarantee, or victualler's recognizance, to ensure that they intended the proper and orderly keeping of such a house.

The earliest surviving recognizances for Hertfordshire date from 1596-7. There are also some from the early seventeenth century but until the nineteenth century very few generally have survived. From 1753, when annual licensing became a statutory requirement, the Clerk of the Peace was required to keep a register of all recognizances entered into; unfortunately these registers for Hertfordshire survive only from 1817.

A list for the county giving names of landlords and inn signs, arranged by parish, between 1806 and 1828 can be found in the Quarter Sessions catalogue at HALS. The recognizances are catalogued under QS Var 15-2655, and include a memorandum of those for 1712 (Odsey Hundred), and recognizances and registers covering 1806 and 1817-28. Hertford Borough alehouse licences and victuallers' recognizances are catalogued under Hertford Corporation Records Volume 19, 1623-1828. Those for the Liberty of St Albans (HALS: LS Var 5-6) date from 1786-90, 1799 and 1815-28; a parish index of landlords' names and inn signs, 1822-8, is in the Quarter Sessions catalogue at HALS.

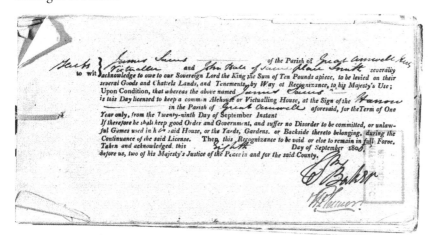

Extract from a victualler's recognizance from Great Amwell, 1806 (Ref. QS Var 368-433 Hertford Hundred).

Between 1830 and 1869, restrictions on the opening of inns and public houses were removed and the JPs' powers to control them were weakened. For this period there is consequently less evidence available for pub licensing.

Licensing laws were again revised by an act of 1872 which set up new licensing committees. Minutes of the County Licensing Committee survive for the periods 1873-94 and 1897-1951, and those of the Liberty of St Albans Licensing Committee from 1873 to 1951. The Petty Sessions registers also start from the date of this act and alehouse licence registers have survived for Barnet 1872-1964 (HALS: PS2/3); Bishop's Stortford 1922-59 (HALS: PS3/3); Buntingford 1946-59 (HALS: PS4/3); Cheshunt 1931-68 (HALS: PS5/3); Dacorum 1876-81, 1901-63 (HALS: PS6/3); Hatfield 1893-1902 (HALS: PS8/3); Hertford Borough 1903-46, 1951-66 (HALS: PS 9/3); Hertford County 1903-46, 1951-66 (HALS: PS 10/3); Hitchin 1872-1953 (HALS: PS12/3); South Mimms 1939-65 (HALS: PS 13/3); Odsey 1872-1953 (HALS: PS14/3); Stevenage 1897-1954 (HALS: PS17/3); Ware 1872-1966 (HALS: PS18/3); Watford 1874-1951 (HALS: PS19/3); Welwyn 1899-1955 (HALS: PS20/3); St Albans City 1900-75 (HALS: PS21/3).

County books that may be helpful include *Hertfordshire Inns* (two volumes) by W. Branch Johnson, Hertfordshire Countryside, 1962-3; revised by Graham Jolliffe and Arthur Jones as *Hertfordshire Inns and Public Houses,* Hertfordshire Publications, 1995.

Suggested further reading
Gibson, J. and Hunter, J., *Victuallers' Licences: Records for Family and Local Historians,* FFHS, 2nd ed, 1997

Licensed tradesmen: badgers and higglers
From 1562 dealers in corn and other commodities were required to apply for a licence from the JPs, whose responsibility it became to regulate their conduct and behaviour. These men were usually itinerant traders, or pedlars, and the licence was an attempt to prevent profiteering or the removal from the county of important foodstuffs at times of hardship.

The Clerk of the Peace was required to keep a register of licences granted. There is no trace of such a record for Hertfordshire before 1686 but there are lists of licences on the Sessions Rolls from 1616 (HALS: HAT/SR 28). Two registers of 'badgers, drovers, kidders and higglers' survive for the periods 1686-1710 and 1765-7 (HALS: QS Var 1 & 2) and have been printed in the published Hertford Quarter Sessions calendars, volumes 6, 7 and 8. There are also many references in the calendars to those who were brought before the JPs for trading without a licence.

Printers
In 1799, when Great Britain was at war with France and there was unease about the possibility of revolutionary activity in this country, all printers were required to declare the existence of their presses to the local Clerk of the Peace. The act was not repealed until 1869.

References to the printers who made that declaration can be found in the published Quarter Sessions calendars, and a list of names is contained in Le Hardy, W., *Guide to the Hertfordshire Record Office,* 1961.

Gamekeepers
The right to kill game was for centuries a closely guarded privilege which required a substantial property qualification or social position. From 1710 the Lord of the Manor could appoint a gamekeeper who had authority to kill game on that manor and whose name had to be registered with the Clerk of the Peace. The gamekeeper's certificate was issued for the fee of one shilling. From 1784 all those qualified by the ownership of property to kill game were also required to have licences. After 1831 game certificates were granted irrespective of property qualification on payment of the appropriate fee.

Registers of gamekeepers' licences and certificates for killing game survive with the Quarter Sessions records (HALS: QS Var 3-11; LS Var 1-4) and name lists have been printed in the published calendars, covering 1711-1860 (parishes within the jurisdiction of the county Quarter Sessions) and 1764-1868 (parishes within the Liberty and Borough of St Albans).

Teachers, surgeons, and midwives

Schoolteachers were strictly regulated by the Church from the earliest times. Prosecutions were brought in the archdeacon's court against teachers for teaching without a licence. The earliest reference amongst the records held at HALS dates from 1569 (HALS: ASA7/8 folio 165), when a George Lewes admitted that he had taught children grammar without a licence. Early surgeons and midwives also required a licence from the ecclesiastical court. Midwives were included because of their power to baptise a newborn child thought unlikely to survive. Testimonials relating to licensing 1686-1709 are included amongst the papers of the Archdeaconry of Huntingdon (HALS: AHH 14/2) and the Archdeaconry of St Albans (HALS: ASA 20B; two testimonials only).

From the seventeenth century references to teachers prosecuted for keeping schools without a bishop's licence can be found in the Quarter Sessions papers (see the index to the published Quarter Sessions calendars).

Background information on schoolteachers in later centuries may be found in the records of the school where they were employed (see Chapter 7, Schools and Education).

From the nineteenth century, medical and other health staff can sometimes be traced through hospital records (see Chapter 6, The Poor and the Sick) and it may be worth consulting administrative records, particularly for senior staff. HALS also holds:

◆ Hill End Hospital: registers of staff 1898-1945 (HALS: Off Acc 1025)
◆ Letchworth Hospital: nurses' address book 1914-55 (HALS: HV5/4A)
◆ Royston Cottage Hospital: staff address books 1924-8 (HALS: HV6/4A)

The London Metropolitan Archives holds staff registers for Leavesden Hospital 1872-1972 and for Shenley Hospital 1942-85.

Police officers

Researching police ancestors in Hertfordshire can be a difficult task, as very few records of use to the genealogist have survived. However, there may be more information for policemen serving in the south of the county, in those parishes covered by the Metropolitan Police force.

The Hertford Borough and St Albans Borough police forces were established in 1836 and, as their names suggest, they were responsible only for the areas within those borough boundaries. The rest of the county had no professional police force until the establishment of the Hertfordshire Police in 1841. In 1877 the St Albans Borough Police became the St Albans City Police, and this force remained independent when in 1889 Hertford Borough and Hertfordshire Police were amalgamated. It was not until 1947 that the City Police force was finally brought into the Hertfordshire Police. The first policewoman joined the force in 1928.

Not all policemen serving in Hertfordshire were employed by one or other of these forces. In 1839 the second Metropolitan Police Act extended the Metropolitan Police District to include the whole of Middlesex and parishes in Hertfordshire, Surrey, Essex and Kent that were wholly or in part within a fifteen-mile radius of Charing Cross.

A policeman by the stocks in Aldbury (Ref. County Views Ald/50).

Where to find the records

Records of serving policemen have not survived well in Hertfordshire and there is a limited amount of material of use to genealogists. HALS holds some material on the Hertfordshire Police, including:

- personnel record sheets of regular and special constables, 1888-1961 (HALS: Off Acc 229). Not a full collection but the surviving sheets give extensive personal and career details of the officers.
- appointments register, 1920-60 (HALS: Off Acc 94). This only lists the surname of the appointee and their year of joining the Hertfordshire Police.
- candidates (constables) book, 1952-63 (HALS: Off Acc 922). The names, addresses, ages, occupations and heights of applicants for the rank of constable are given.

Books that may be useful for background information include Osborn, N., *The story of Hertfordshire Police,* Hertfordshire Countryside, 1969, and Pringle, N. and Treversh, J., *150 years of policing in Watford District and Hertfordshire County,* Radley Shaw, 1991.

The records of the Metropolitan Police are held at the Public Record Office (PRO: MEPO). These are quite extensive and include registers going back to 1829. The PRO has a useful leaflet guide to finding Metropolitan Police Records of Service.

Suggested further reading

Shearman, A., *My ancestor was a policeman,* Society of Genealogists, 2000

Parish and union officers

An ancestor who was employed by the parish or by the local Board of Guardians can often be traced through the records created by those bodies.

It will, of course, be necessary to know the name of the parish or union concerned and the approximate dates of employment, but with these it may be possible to build up a picture of their working life and the duties they undertook.

References to officers can be found within the parish records, including vestry minutes and the various account books (HALS: DP), and the Petty and Quarter Sessions records (HALS: PS and QS). Amongst the Quarter Sessions papers, for instance, are lists of parish constables appointed at various petty sessional meetings and returned to the Clerk of the Peace 1845-70 (HALS: QSCb 38).

Local newspapers will often contain quite detailed reports of meetings of Boards of Guardians, with reference to such staff as the workhouse master or mistress. Town directories may list local officials.

Within the papers of the Boards of Guardians held at HALS are registers of staff service for Berkhamsted Union 1896-1930 (HALS: BG/BER 30-32); Hemel Hempstead 1876-1930 (HALS: BG/HEM 20-21) and Ware 1873, 1896-1932 (HALS: BG/WAR 38-41).

Clergymen

There are both published and archival sources for tracing clerical ancestors in Hertfordshire. The evidence which survives within the appropriate church should also not be forgotten, which may include a listing of clergy associated with the parish, memorial inscriptions and so on.

Clergyman and workmen at Therfield Church 1875 (Ref. County Views Ther/5).

The ecclesiastical records held at HALS may be useful in tracing the career of an individual clergyman although there will be little personal information included:

♦ the ordination of priests within the diocese 1877-1986 (HALS:DSA 1/2)

♦ ordination registers 1896-1919 (HALS:D/ACC 607)

♦ curates' licences assigning them to serve within a particular parish c.1574-1639 (HALS:ASA 26; DSA 1/3)

♦ institutions of priests to benefices 1846-1963 (HALS:DSA 1/1; DSA 1/6)

♦ induction mandates 1554-1972 (HALS:AHH 1; ASA 1; ASA 6; ASA 26; DSA 1/13)

- non-residence licences for priests and curates residing outside of the parish 1887-1951 (HALS:DSA 1/4)
- resignation from benefices 1896-1917 (HALS:DSA 1/7)

Published sources at HALS include *Crockford's Clerical Directory* (copies from 1829); the *Hertfordshire Almanac* 1849-1920 (this contains lists of incumbents, curates and patrons over a period not covered by the diocesan directories) and *St Albans Directory and Year Books* 1892 to date (includes useful personnel information by parish). It may also be useful to consult the published lists of graduates from Oxford and Cambridge universities, *Alumni Oxonienses* and *Alumni Cantabrigienses,* from before 1500 to 1886 (Oxford) and 1900 (Cambridge).

In 1851 an ecclesiastical census was taken of the whole country and the returns for Hertfordshire have been published as *Religion in Hertfordshire 1847-1851,* edited by Judith Berg, Hertfordshire Record Society, 1995. The entries give a useful summary of the religious situation in each parish and often include comments about individual clergymen.

Estate workers and servants
It will usually be very difficult to trace servants, except when they appear in the national census returns. However, some estate workers and indoor servants may be identified in estate account and wages books, where these survive.

Some of the large estates in Hertfordshire have deposited records at HALS though few of these will be relevant to the search for working ancestors. Consulting the full catalogue of estate papers will help family historians identify what is available. A selection of possible sources includes:

- Gorhambury household wages book 1771-94 (HALS: XI/62)
- Gorhambury estate wages book 1849-90 (HALS: XI/119)
- Watton Woodhall estate wages book 1789 (HALS: DE/B1297/E2)
- Ashridge estate workbook 1850-2 (HALS: DE/LS/B144)
- Panshanger estate account and wage books 1691-1710; 1762-4; 1736-42; 1779-87 (HALS: DE/P/A)
- Great Gaddesden estate account and wage books 1804-14; 1839-49 (HALS: DE/Hl/E1-4)

Other estate papers may still be in private hands and are not usually available to researchers. Enquiries about records held at Hatfield House may be addressed in writing to the estate archivist.

Brewers and maltsters
Brewing and malting have been important activities in Hertfordshire from the earliest times and malting is one of its oldest industries, concentrated particularly in the east of the county.

The brewery papers held at HALS (HALS: DE) normally consist of title deeds and business papers which may be of little help to family historians. A useful name list of brewers in the county can be found in Poole, H., *Here for the beer: A gazetteer of the brewers of Hertfordshire,* Watford Museum, 1984. Small brewers who were also publicans can be traced through victuallers' recognizances (see above).

Some early 'maltmen' are included by name in the lists of licences granted to badgers and higglers by Quarter Sessions from 1616 (HALS: HAT/SR 28).

Maltings at Sawbridgeworth (Ref. Local Studies collection).

For background information on the industry see Clark, C., *The British malting industry since 1830,* Hambledon Press, 1998, or Mathias, P., *The brewing industry in England 1700-1830,*Cambridge University Press, 1959.

Richmond, L. & Turton, A., *The brewing industry: a guide to historical records,* Manchester University Press, 1990, is a useful guide to the whereabouts of brewery archives.

Apprenticeship
Apprenticeship records can be of great value, indicating the trade or occupation followed by an ancestor in later life, as well as the names of his or her master and sponsor.

Apprenticeship Indenture for John Webster dated 1831 (Ref. 28879).

A searchable database of poor law apprenticeship indentures from the early seventeenth century to the early nineteenth century, with currently over 1,700 entries, is available for consultation at HALS. The original documents are among the poor law records, catalogued by parish (HALS:DP). An indenture was the formal agreement drawn up between the employer and the apprentice or his or her parents or guardians; it was so named because the document was cut in two along an irregular line (indented), making fraud impossible because the two edges would always match.

Registers of apprenticeships for St Albans are available on microfilm at HALS for the periods 1628-30, 1697-1730 and 1732-1805 (HALS: Off Acc 1162 Nos 286, 287 and 927). Hertford Borough records include apprenticeship documents 1630-1845 (HALS: HB Volume 26).

Company archives held at HALS

Some companies have deposited their archives at HALS although in most cases there is little held about individual employees and they are therefore of limited use for family historians.

Amongst the deposited papers held at HALS (HALS: DE) are the following for two local companies:

◆ John Dickinson & Co. Ltd (HALS: DE/Di). Papermaking has long been an important industry in Hertfordshire and the firm of John Dickinson was at the forefront of innovation. The deposited archives are quite extensive but there is limited information on individual members of staff (HALS: DE/Di/1/7; DE/Di/1/10/57-62 and DE/Di/3/6 contain matters related to staff and employment). The apprenticeship indenture of Frederick Barlow, 1858, survives (HALS: DE/Dk/B1). See Evans, J., *The endless web: John Dickinson & Co. Ltd 1804-1954,* Jonathan Cape, 1955, for background information on the company and lists of some staff members.

◆ Addis Ltd (HALS: ACC 3168, 3193). The papers from this famous brushmaking firm include some staff time and wage books for the periods 1905-7, 1914-16, 1929, 1931, 1938-52. See also Beaver, P., *Addis 1780-1980: All about the home,* Publications for Companies, 1980.

Other Hertfordshire occupations and industries

Hertfordshire has had a great diversity of other occupations and industries, many of which have left behind them little in the way of documentary archive evidence.

Museums and books of local history may therefore be extremely useful to family historians, particularly for craft occupations such as straw plaiting. There are also many published books relating to local firms and industries, such as aircraft development at de Havilland and British Aerospace or the film and television industry, that can be consulted at HALS and in local libraries. Reference can be made to the Hertfordshire library catalogue (available online at <www.hertsdirect.org>).

Chapter 5

Crime and punishment

If an ancestor was involved in a crime, whether as the accused, the victim or a witness, the records of the proceedings of the criminal courts can provide a fascinating insight into everyday life, as well as such valuable information as a physical description and a verbatim report of what they had to say. After sentencing criminals may have spent time in one of the county's gaols, or been transported to the colonies. The records of the courts whose work is described in this chapter have not always survived (and court records less than thirty years old are not open for public inspection) but time spent in researching this subject may be well rewarded.

The Assize courts

The assizes were the principal criminal courts in the country from the thirteenth century until their abolition in 1971. The assize judges dealt with a wide range of serious cases and an ancestor coming before this court for certain crimes could face the death penalty or transportation for life.

The Courts of Assize were responsible for trying offences, such as murder, rape, robbery or arson, which were too serious to be dealt with at Quarter Sessions (see below). In the thirteenth century two judges were commissioned to act as the king's justices, travelling from the High Court in London on a circuit from one major town to another. England and Wales were divided up into six circuits (London and Middlesex were excluded). Hertfordshire belonged to the Home Circuit which also included Essex, Kent, Surrey and Sussex. In 1875 the Home Circuit was abolished and replaced by a South-Eastern Circuit which included Hertfordshire, Essex, Kent, Surrey, Sussex, Huntingdonshire, Cambridgeshire, Norfolk and Suffolk. In 1971 the Assize courts were merged with the courts of Quarter Sessions to form the new Crown courts.

Twice a year, two justices from the central criminal courts in London would travel the circuit, taking gaol delivery (i.e. trying prisoners) at various points in the counties within it and hearing cases considered to be too serious for

Quarter Sessions. In the main, the Hertford Assize courts sat at Hertford .

Unfortunately, since the assizes were not strictly a local court nor part of the centralised court system in London, they were by their nature always on the move and the records have suffered in consequence. Unlike other courts traditionally housed in a fixed location, assize records were not continually in the custody of one person or place, and tended to be transferred between justices or their clerks, and were therefore prone to accidental loss or destruction. The clerk of the Midland Circuit in 1800, for instance, is believed to have been responsible for the loss of anything pre-dating the nineteenth century for that circuit.

The Old Bailey Sessions Proceedings, the accounts of trials held at London's central criminal court,1674-1834, have been made available as a searchable text online and free of charge at <www.oldbaileyonline.org>. This joint project between the Universities of Hertfordshire and Sheffield makes it easy to discover whether Hertfordshire ancestors are among the several hundred thousand individuals who were tried or gave evidence across the county boundary.

Where to find the records

The records of the Home Circuit contain the earliest surviving files of any circuit, dating from 1559. They are held at the Public Record Office (PRO: ASSI) and include indictments (charges) and depositions (sworn evidence), amongst other records. Before 1733 most of the records are in Latin. To find a particular case, you will need to know the name of the accused and the date of the trial. Those for the period 1559-1624 have been listed and indexed in Cockburn, J.S., *Calendars of Assize Records – Home Circuit Indictments Elizabeth I and James I*, HMSO, 1975.

At HALS, the papers of the county sheriffs (HALS: SH) contain several assize documents, including trial calendars 1817-1931 (HALS: SH4/1). The sheriff was responsible for preparing these calendars, which listed the prisoners and the crimes for which they were to be tried as well as jurors and officials.

Local newspapers are extremely useful when researching nineteenth century assize records. Verbatim reports of trials are common and will, in many cases, give more information of use to the family historian than will be found in the official records. *The Hertfordshire Almanac* (see Chapter 9) lists dates of court sittings.

Quarter Sessions

The records of the courts of Quarter Sessions contain vast amounts of information useful to the family historian, whether an ancestor was a petty criminal or brought up before the magistrates for failing to perform his statutory duty in maintaining the highways, presented in a bastardy case or simply seeking a licence to carry out his trade.

The first Commission for Keeping the Peace in Hertfordshire was granted in 1327 and from 1350 the court of Quarter Sessions met four times a year. It was not only a court of law but, from the late fourteenth century until well into the nineteenth century, carried out many local administrative functions and became the seat of government authority over the county. From 1461 the Justices of the Peace (JPs) gradually assumed more and more administrative responsibilities. The criminal cases dealt with by Quarter Sessions could include serious offences such as riot, assault, theft or poaching, but were not capital offences demanding the death penalty which had to be adjourned to the assizes. Courts of Quarter Sessions could, however, sentence an offender to transportation, imprisonment, branding or whipping.

Hertfordshire was divided between four separate courts of Quarter Sessions. The general Hertford County Sessions carried out the bulk of the work but the Liberty of St Albans Quarter Sessions had jurisdiction over twenty-four parishes in the west of the county. In addition, the two ancient chartered boroughs in the county, Hertford and St Albans, each held their own courts. When searching for evidence of an ancestor amongst Quarter Sessions records it is important to know in which parish he or she lived in order to find the court before which they might have appeared.

The JPs met quarterly. The amount of work they dealt with was such that from the early sixteenth century they were also allowed to attend to minor matters by meeting between Quarter Sessions, leading to the development of the courts of Petty Sessions (see below).

In 1835, following the passing of the reforming Municipal Corporations Act, the two borough Quarter Sessions courts were abolished. In 1874 the two surviving courts were amalgamated to form a single court of Quarter Sessions with an eastern and western division. Further social and administrative reforms meant that many of the functions formerly carried out by the Quarter Sessions were gradually transferred to new bodies and in 1889, all remaining administrative responsibilities were assumed by the newly-formed county councils, leaving the Quarter Sessions a purely judicial court. Courts of Quarter Sessions were finally abolished in 1971 when they were replaced by the new Crown court system.

Where to find the records
The official record of the work undertaken by the courts of Quarter Sessions is contained within the Quarter Sessions rolls:
◆ County sessions 1588-1971 (HALS: QSR)
◆ Liberty of St Albans sessions: 1758-1874 (HALS: LSR)
◆ Borough of St Albans sessions: 1784-1836 (HALS: Off Acc 1162, nos 407A-607)
◆ Borough of Hertford sessions: 1605-1835 (HALS: HB)

These, and the sessions books which accompany them, contain such details as presentments (statements on oath) and indictments (charges).

The most frequent subjects covered include assault, theft, trespass, game offences, breaking and entering, disorderly behaviour, slander, failure to perform highway duty, encroachment on common land or rights of way, failure to clear ditches, absence from church and Sabbath-breaking, unlawful assembly, weights and measures offences and unlicensed trading. There are also depositions relating to particular cases, criminal or otherwise, and occasionally the final order of the court. Invariably, the rolls also include recognizances (bonds of guarantee) for the binding over of offenders or for ensuring that witnesses appear before the court to give evidence.

The records of the Quarter Sessions held at HALS are extensive and space does not allow more than a brief description of the different types of document produced by the courts. However, of greater immediate use to the family historian is the series of published calendars to the papers, which are indexed and are available at HALS and through the library service (see Chapter 9, Printed Sources). Newspaper reports are also a good source for court proceedings. The *Hertfordshire Almanac* (see Chapter 9) lists dates of court sittings and names of JPs.

Petty Sessions

As with the other courts, family historians will find the Petty Sessions records of great use if their ancestor was ever brought before the justices for a minor matter.

Extract from a conviction book, 1830 (Ref. QSCB/1).

Name.	Residence, &c.	Date of Conviction.	Offence.	Punishment.
Horwood Jane	Berkhamstead	21st Sept. 1830	injuring a Jail	Fine 1s
Shatton William	Hemel Hempstead	4th Oct.	Stealing Pears	1 Month hard labour
Slopen George	Hamstead	11th August	damaging Wheat	Fine 6d
Brooks John	Wigginton	17th August	Cutting a Tree	Fine £5
White William	Bishops Stortford	3rd Sept.	damage a Building	Fine 1/3
Hudgell Stephen				
Gunn James and Kidd John	Great Hallingbury	1st Oct.	stealing Fruit	2 Months hard labour

These courts developed from early in the sixteenth century, when JPs were required occasionally to meet in their own parts of the county, outside the Quarter Sessions, to deal with certain administrative matters or minor offences. In time, these meetings were formalised as Petty Sessions.

Prior to the nineteenth century, only rarely is there a mention of the areas or 'divisions' on which this organisation was based and it was not unusual for JPs to use their own homes as a makeshift courtroom. In Hertfordshire, records of this early period have not survived. In 1848 the duties of the justices were more clearly set out and in 1855 the Criminal Justice Act established the terms of their summary jurisdiction. People charged with thefts of a low value and other minor offences could be convicted by two justices in an open court, with the right of appeal to the Quarter Sessions, and convictions, depositions and other records had to be returned to the Clerk of the Peace for filing with the Quarter Sessions records. The necessity of filing formal convictions with the Clerk of the Peace was not removed until the Criminal Justice Administration Act of 1914.

Where to find the records
Divisional boundaries were often indistinct and there were many changes in the composition of the Petty Sessional divisions over the eighteenth and nineteenth centuries. Maps and details of the parishes in each division can be found in the catalogue to the Petty Sessions at HALS (HALS: PS): Albury Division; Chipping Barnet Division; Bishop's Stortford Division; Buntingford Division; Cheshunt Division; Dacorum Division; Eastwick Division; Hatfield Division; Hertford Borough Division; Hertford County Division; Hertford and Ware Division; Hitchin Division; South Mimms Division; Odsey Division; St Albans County Division; Shenley Division; Stevenage Division; Ware Division; Watford Division; Welwyn Division; St Albans City Division.

Many notices of conviction sent to the Clerk of the Peace will be found on the sessions rolls of the Quarter Sessions (and are therefore to be found in the published calendars, see Chapter 9). These date from the mid-seventeenth century and include convictions under the Conventicle Act 1664 for attending nonconformist services, and various offences connected with the maintenance and repair of highways (HALS: QSR 15, 22). A register of convictions of profane swearers survives for the period 1695-1705 (HALS: QS Misc 1471); under an act of 1694 persons swearing or cursing profanely could be convicted by a JP.

With respect to the nineteenth century, material received from the Petty Sessional divisions themselves includes court registers, court minutes, and fines and fees accounts, mainly from the late 1800s onwards. These records are supplemented by thirty-one bound volumes of convictions and depositions (1868-1913) filed with the Clerk of the Peace (HALS: QSC 1-7; 10-33). Registers also survive for the period 1855-1917 which may be used as indexes to the bound convictions (HALS: QSC 37-43, LS Var 11).

Juvenile offenders
Records of conviction under the Juvenile Offenders Act (1847) and the Summary Jurisdiction Act (1879) were also to be returned to the Clerk of the Peace and these, together with depositions, are bound into five volumes covering the period 1857-1913 (HALS: QSC 8-9; 34-36). Two registers for the same period (HALS: QSC 42-43) can be used as indexes to these volumes. Some earlier juvenile convictions are also to be found in the bundles mentioned above and these records provide the earliest information so far available in HALS relating to juvenile crime in Hertfordshire.

HALS holds records for the Hertfordshire Reformatory School (later the Hertfordshire Training School), Chapmore End, Bengeo, for the period 1857-1973. Access is restricted for fifty years from the last date in each volume, and those documents currently open for research include log books 1892-1901 and 1914-51 (HALS: DE/Hts/Q18-21); admission registers 1857-1949 (HALS: DE/Hts/Q25-32) and registers of boys discharged or released on licence 1876-1948 (HALS: DE/Hts/Q36-47). The JPs were also able, from 1857, to send children in need of care and protection to an industrial school to learn a trade; attendance registers 1842-7 and 1850-7 survive for the King's Langley School of Industry (HALS: HEd1/195/1-2). The industrial school at Leavesden was managed by the St Pancras Board of Guardians and related records are held by the London Metropolitan Archives.

Hertfordshire's gaols

Once a prisoner had been committed to gaol, it becomes harder for a family historian to discover details of their movements and experiences. Many of the appropriate records have not survived, though with luck some information can still be found.

Shenley lock-up around the 1960s (Ref. Local Studies collection).

Until the reforms of the early nineteenth century, prisons were terrible places, mostly unvisited by magistrates and run by gaolers who demanded fees for virtually all the necessities of life and could often be cruel and sadistic. Epidemics regularly decimated the prison population and sometimes those who came into contact with them in court.

Fees were abolished by statute in 1815 and the 1823 and 1835 Prisons Acts did something to improve conditions. JPs were then compelled to take their duties towards prisoners more seriously and send in annual returns to central government. Under an act of 1877 all prisons came under the control of the Home Office and prison conditions and discipline were standardised throughout the country.

Each parish originally had some form of lock-up or cage which could hold an offender overnight before being taken before the justices in the morning. A good example still survives at Shenley. Under Tudor and Stuart acts concerning the poor law, houses of correction were set up throughout the county to detain and set to work 'vagabonds and other idle persons'; they housed vagrants, petty criminals and some prisoners on remand. These were administered by the JPs but by the nineteenth century they differed little from the prisons. No records survive at HALS specifically for those who suffered these forms of imprisonment.

The county gaol was situated in Hertford, in the castle during the Middle Ages and later in the town. It was closed and the prison building sold off in 1879. The High Sheriff was responsible for the custody and production of prisoners for trial and for their punishment, but from 1531 the JPs in Quarter Sessions were responsible for the provision and maintenance of the county gaol.

The other main prison was the St Albans Liberty gaol, situated in the Abbey Gatehouse from the sixteenth century to the 1860s. A new prison was built on the outskirts of the town in 1869 but this closed in 1915.

Prisoners tried in the county and given the death sentence were executed in Hertfordshire until the closure of St Albans prison. The burial place will not normally be known, as bodies were frequently buried nearby the gallows, in unconsecrated ground. The bodies of four executed criminals originally buried within the grounds of St Albans prison between 1869 and its closure, were removed and reinterred in St Albans cemetery when the prison building was disposed of in 1931.

Following the closure of the prison at St Albans, other arrangements had to be made for prisoners convicted at Hertfordshire courts. Pentonville Prison received male prisoners from the Hertford Assizes and the Quarter Sessions, the Boroughs of Hertford and St Albans (City), and Petty Sessions at Barnet, Cheshunt, Dacorum, Hatfield, Hertford, Watford, St Albans and Ware. Prisoners from Petty Sessions at Bishop's Stortford, Buntingford, Albury and Odsey went to Cambridge prison. From Petty Sessions at Hitchin, Stevenage and Welwyn, they were sent to Bedford prison. Female prisoners were sent to Holloway prison.

Where to find the records

No prison-related records survive at HALS before about 1800. The names and details of some prisoners may, however, be found in the Quarter Sessions rolls, as prison inspection (and investigation of complaints), and records of the costs of providing medicines or transporting prisoners came within the jurisdiction of the JPs. Names of prison staff may also be found here. Other records at HALS include:

◆ Governors' journals 1834-78, Hertford Gaol. These six volumes record the names of prisoners who were singled out for punishment or other notice (HALS: QS Gaol).

◆ Gaol papers St Albans and Hertford 1853, 1888 (HALS: QS Misc B47/1, 51/13, 58/10). These contain some calendars of prisoners, giving names and dates of offences.

◆ Gaol calendar 1894-1928 (HALS: QS records)

◆ Gaol books 1770-1828 (HALS: LSGB 1-4) and recognizance books 1829-94 (HALS: LSRB 1-3) for the Liberty of St Albans

◆ Assignments of county gaol and inmates 1798-1865 (HALS: SH 2/2/1,2). As the outgoing sheriff handed over to his successor, the names of prisoners awaiting trial were listed together with their offences.

◆ County court registers 1825-57 (HALS: SH 3/1/1-18 and Off Acc 1162). The names of plaintiffs and defendants in cases of debt are recorded, including the sums to be repaid.

Records relating to prisons and prisoners may also be found at the PRO (PRO: HO or PCOM), or in neighbouring county record offices, e.g. Bedfordshire and Luton Archives and Record Service for records of Bedford gaol.

Suggested further reading
Hawkings, D.T., *Criminal ancestors: a guide to historical criminal records in England and Wales,* Alan Sutton, 1992.

Transportation

Although the majority of transportation sentences were issued by the assizes, all four of the courts of Quarter Sessions within the county had the power to do so. When an ancestor is found to have been transported, a wealth of information can sometimes be found on him or her, detailed within the records of the relevant court.

Transportation emerged from the practices of banishing religious dissidents from the country and coercing vagrants into military service as an alternative to being whipped. It was first inflicted as a punishment in 1597, as a cheaper solution to dealing with the overcrowding of English prisons, and as a means of applying mercy to those convicts sentenced to death. It was also seen as a deterrent to other would-be criminals, and as a supply of cheap labour for the emerging colonies.

When transportation was first introduced, most convicts were transported to the American colonies, but also to others such as Bermuda and Antigua. The outbreak of the American War of Independence meant transportation there inevitably ceased, and from 1787 convicts were shipped to the new penal colony at Botany Bay, New South Wales, instead, expanding to other parts of Australia until 1868 when transportation ended.

In total, approximately 50,000 convicts were transported to America, of whom fewer than 500 were from Hertfordshire. Between 1787 and 1867 over 160,000 convicts were transported to Australia from the British Isles (including Ireland), about 1,300 of them from Hertfordshire. The majority were men who were taken to prison hulks moored either on the Thames or at Portsmouth to await shipment or to serve their sentence on the hulks doing public works. Women were transported separately from 1805 and were held in prison. Transportation was initially to New South Wales and then to Tasmania. From 1852 all convicts were sent to Western Australia.

Where to find the records

Knowing which court would have tried your ancestor, and correspondingly where any surviving records might be found, can be problematical. Fortunately, a great deal of work has been done in recent years in bringing together all the sources relating to transported Hertfordshire convicts, enabling family historians to track down a transported ancestor with relative ease.

The following two publications should be the starting-point for any search and will avoid the need for lengthy searches through the court records:

◆ Griffin, K., *Hertfordshire criminals sentenced to be transported to America* is a draft alphabetical listing of Hertfordshire convicts sent to America, available at HALS.

◆ Griffin, K., *Transported beyond the seas. An alphabetical listing of criminals prosecuted in Hertfordshire who received transportation sentences to Australia 1784-1866,* Hertfordshire Family History Society, Special Publication no. 1, 1997. Available at HALS and through inter-library loan. This is an alphabetical listing of all criminals (1,915 in total) prosecuted in Hertfordshire who received transportation sentences between 1784 and 1866. It gives the criminal's age and place of residence (where known), the court and the date of trial, the sentence, the place and the details of the crime and all the victims. All criminals are traced to either transportation to Australia, Bermuda or Gibraltar or to being signed up for the army, pardoned, dying or just simply escaping.

Having consulted the indexes to these publications, it should be possible to accurately pinpoint which records need to be consulted in order to gain more information about the particular case. The sources used for the above publications are held at the Public Record Office (Assize, Home Office and Admiralty records) and at HALS (Quarter Sessions records for the Hertford Borough, St Albans Borough, St Albans Liberty, and County Sessions). Local newspapers will also be useful in filling in background information.

Chapter 6
The poor and the sick

Before the sixteenth century relief of poverty was largely the responsibility of the church or the manor and, in boroughs, gilds and municipal corporations. Potential sources for this early period are manorial or charity records. It is the old and the new poor laws, however, that most genealogists will encounter, as well as the institutions, including hospitals, in existence just prior to the setting up of the Welfare State in the 1940s. The records that have been created since the end of the sixteenth century may yield information about the humblest of ancestors. Amongst the most difficult people to trace are those who moved about the country, such as Gypsies and itinerant workers, and some suggestions are offered that may guide genealogists to useful sources.

The poor law
What is generally referred to as 'the poor law' was in fact a large body of legislation that extended from the time of the Tudors to 1948. The different records that these many acts created can be of great interest to family historians as they touched the lives of the great majority of our ancestors. In Hertfordshire their survival has been relatively poor but most parishes will be found to have at least some records.

The old poor law was created by a series of acts passed during the sixteenth century and consolidated in 1598 and 1601, establishing the parish as the unit of administration and introducing compulsory, rate-financed poor relief. A distinction was made from the beginning between the 'deserving' and 'undeserving' poor (the latter being those who could, but would not, work, i.e. vagrants and beggars) and the poor law was seen as a safety net for those for whom the available charity resources were inadequate. Parish officers, including overseers of the poor, were appointed by the vestry and the account books of the overseers may contain information on payments made to named individuals. This system continued in place, with some amendments, for the next 200 years.

Severe economic and social distress in the early decades of the nineteenth century highlighted the abuses and inadequacies of the old poor law. In 1832 the government set up a Royal Commission to investigate the poor law system thoroughly, and the Poor Law Amendment Act was passed in 1834. Three Poor Law Commissioners were appointed and the country was divided into unions of parishes. Each parish in the union elected one or more guardians of the poor who met weekly or fortnightly to conduct business. Many features of the old system continued under the new poor law.

In Hertfordshire, the act created thirteen unions: Barnet, Berkhamsted, Bishop's Stortford, Buntingford, Hatfield, Hemel Hempstead, Hertford, Hitchin, Royston, St Albans, Ware, Watford, Welwyn. The area covered by the unions sometimes crossed county boundaries. In Hertfordshire this meant that Cheshunt was part of the Edmonton Union, and that the Barnet Union included some Middlesex parishes, Bishop's Stortford Union some Essex parishes, Berkhamsted Union some Buckinghamshire parishes, and the Royston Union some Cambridgeshire parishes. Union boundaries were later often used for civil registration districts and census enumerators' boundaries (see map, pages 10-11).

The new poor law officially came to an end in March 1930, when the unions ceased to exist, but there was a curious hybrid period until July 1948 when the relief of poverty was the responsibility of county and county borough councils (see below).

Because the poor had to be supported by local rates paid by the better-off inhabitants, efforts were made from a very early date to discourage strangers entering a parish who might need parish relief. The 1662 Act of Settlement introduced 'settlement certificates' for migrant workers and from 1697 the poor had to have a certificate to enter any new parish. This became the most common poor law document, setting out the rights of an individual or family to settle in a particular parish. If they subsequently became 'chargeable' in another parish, their parish of settlement would accept them back and provide for them. The conditions for settlement changed with time but could be gained by, for example, birth, apprenticeship, working in a parish for over one year, serving in a parish office or paying the parish rate. An individual could have more than one settlement during his or her life and it was the most recent one that was valid at any particular time. Women took their husband's settlement on marriage. The certificate, to be valid, had to be signed by the churchwardens as well as the overseers of the poor, attested by two witnesses and approved by two magistrates.

A 'removal order' would be issued if someone 'intruded' into a parish where he or she then became chargeable, and they would be ordered to be removed to their parish of settlement. Removal could be suspended and sometimes the back of the document will be endorsed with this information. A 'settlement examination' is the potted biography of a pauper, drawn up at this time to determine where he or she had a settlement. The biographical information can be invaluable to a family historian. However, in Hertfordshire the survival of examinations is comparatively rare.

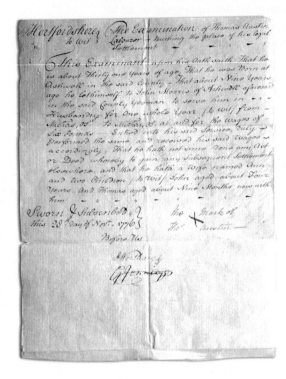

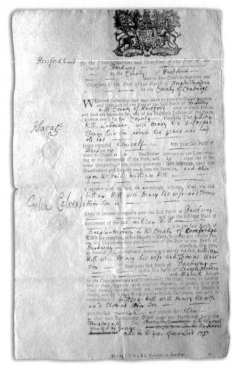

Above left
A settlement examination for Thomas Austin, Ashwell 1776 (Ref. DP/13/13/3).

Above right
A removal order for William Hill, his wife Mary and son Thomas, from Barkway to Steeple Morden, 1737 (Ref. DP/13/13/1).

Originally an illegitimate child gained a settlement in the place where he or she was born, but an act of 1744 changed this to the child taking the mother's settlement. An earlier act of 1733 forced a woman pregnant with a potential bastard to declare the fact and name the father; a man charged on oath with being the father was to be apprehended and committed to gaol unless he agreed to be responsible for any costs. 'Bastardy bonds' and 'filiation orders' serve the same purpose, although they are slightly different documents. Other documents relating to bastardy include 'warrants' for arrests of suspected fathers and 'bastardy examinations'.

There were workhouses for the able-bodied poor in some towns in the sixteenth century but more were erected under acts of 1722 and 1782. The latter, Gilbert's Act, allowed parishes to group together to maintain a shared workhouse if they wished and also for the first time to create separate accommodation for the sick. They tended to become a home for long-term and difficult cases, which was not the original intention; young, deserted, unmarried or widowed mothers, and the aged, were the largest groups in most workhouses and able-bodied males were rarely found there. Records for these early workhouses rarely survive. After 1834 each poor law union had its own workhouse, an intentionally forbidding place that was meant to discourage the able-bodied from seeking relief, except as a place of last resort. The principal record for a union workhouse was the admission and discharge register but, sadly, very few survive in Hertfordshire. Many union workhouses became hospitals after 1930.

The Relieving Officer was responsible for dispensing 'outdoor relief' to those who needed it; his records will include registers, report books and accounts.

The pauper 'apprenticeship indenture' is identical to any other apprenticeship indenture, with the exception that the names of the churchwardens and overseers of the poor are given in place of the parent or guardian. Apprenticeship continued under the new poor law, despite attempts to curtail or stop the system altogether (see Chapter 4).

Extract from the Hatfield workhouse admission register, 1859 (Ref. BG/HAT 45).

Where to find the records

Some Hertfordshire parishes have a good collection of old poor law documents (e.g. Cheshunt) but overall the survival in the county is patchy. Those records deposited at HALS will be found listed with other parish material in the relevant parish catalogue (HALS: DP/.../11-18). Work is ongoing on the production of a searchable computer database.

A name index to settlement certificates from the late seventeenth century to the early nineteenth century held at HALS has been published by the Hertfordshire Family History Society, to be followed by removal orders and examinations. There is also parish poor law material in the Quarter Sessions rolls; the published calendars are name-indexed.

Plan of Bishop's Stortford workhouse (Ref. PC237).

The records of the unions of the new poor law are catalogued at HALS under Boards of Guardians as follows: BG, followed by a three-letter code for the union, e.g. BG/HIT for Hitchin. Cheshunt came within the Edmonton Union, now within the London Borough of Enfield, and the poor law records post-1834 are held by the London Metropolitan Archives.

Many of the main poor law documents of interest to family historians are being filmed for easy access at HALS. In addition to the board minutes for each union, these include:

- Barnet Union: workhouse master's report 1852-63 (HALS: BG/BAR 78-82); workhouse diary 1836-8 (HALS: 70876; extracts from this were published in Kingsford, P. and Jones, A., *Down and out in Hertfordshire*, Hertfordshire Publications, 1984); register of paupers for whom places in service provided 1836-79 (HALS: BG/BAR 83); register of non-resident poor 1920-30 (HALS: BG/BAR 76); register of removal orders 1925-9 (HALS: BG/BAR 77)

- Hatfield Union: workhouse admission and discharge registers 1836-1918 (HALS: BG/HAT 41-54); registers of births in the workhouse 1847-1910 (HALS: BG/HAT 55-56); registers of deaths in the workhouse 1846-1910 (HALS: BG/HAT 57-58); creed registers 1886-1915 (HALS: BG/HAT 60-61)

- Hertford Union: workhouse admission and discharge registers 1873-1916 (HALS: BG/HER 27-38); register of births in the workhouse 1847-1918 (HALS: BG/HER 39); register of deaths in the workhouse 1847-1919 (HALS: BG/HER 40-42); applications for outdoor relief 1876-85 (HALS: BG/HER 45-57)

- Hitchin Union: settlement examinations 1854-60 (HALS: BG/HIT 105); removal orders 1869-95 (HALS: BG/HIT 219); outdoor relief register 1836 (HALS: BG/HIT 109); applications for outdoor relief 1894-1907 (HALS: BG/HIT 110-111, 220)

- Royston Union: register of births in the workhouse 1866-1929 (HALS: BG/ROY 31); register of deaths in the workhouse 1866-1915 (HALS: BG/ROY 32)

- St Albans Union: workhouse admission and discharge registers 1835-54, 1900-31 (HALS: Off Acc 1162); register of births in the workhouse 1871-1952 (HALS: Off Acc 1162); register of deaths in the workhouse 1905-1958 (HALS: Off Acc 1162)

- Ware Union: removal orders 1879-1927 (HALS: BG/WAR 55); workhouse admission and discharge registers 1879-1921 (HALS: BG/WAR 77-78, 109-114); register of births in the workhouse 1905-14 (HALS: BG/WAR 79); register of inmates 1890-1940 (HALS: HSS 3/5/94); creed registers 1919-56 (HALS: HSS 3/5/97-98); register of non-settled and non-resident poor 1921-6 (HALS: BG/WAR 51); applications for outdoor relief 1925-30 (HALS: BG/WAR 104-108)

- Welwyn Union: workhouse admission register 1910-21 (HALS: BG/WEL 16); register of births in the workhouse 1909-16 (HALS: BG/WEL 17); registers of deaths in the workhouse 1907-21 (HALS: BG/WEL 18-19); creed register 1893-1921 (HALS: BG/WEL 20)

Inmates of the union workhouses will be found listed in the ten-yearly census returns from 1841 (see Chapter 3).

Because the new poor law was organised centrally, there is further material in the Public Record Office of local interest; it will be found in the Ministry of Health (PRO: MH) series. These are the records of the Poor Law Commission and the Poor Law Board. Class MH12 contains correspondence which may include details of individuals but is listed by poor law union only with no index of names or subjects.

Suggested further reading
Cole, A., *An introduction to poor law before 1834,* FFHS, 2nd ed., 2000
Fowler, S., *Using poor law records,* PRO, 2001

Public Assistance 1930-48

The records of the poor in the 1930s and 1940s are often overlooked but can be of great help to family historians. Covering a period when electoral registers barely survive, or indeed were not even produced, they can confirm a person's age or address, names of relatives, burial details, and date or cause of death.

In 1930 the Boards of Guardians were abolished and their functions and the whole administration of the poor law was transferred to county and county borough councils (although there were no county borough councils in Hertfordshire) under the general control of the Ministry of Health. The National Assistance Board was set up in 1934, with the general task of providing poor relief. It was not until 1948 that the Welfare State came into existence.

Hertfordshire County Council established a Public Assistance Committee and the county was divided into seven areas, based on the now superseded poor law unions. The scheme was administered by Area Guardians Committees with Relieving Officers in charge of each district.

The Guardians Committees were responsible for a wide variety of poor relief. They took over the institutions and some also ran hospitals or infirmaries. In an attempt to reduce the stigma of the workhouse, the old institutions were all given individual names; in practice, however, the categories of poor housed there remained much the same and included the elderly, the homeless, infants and other persons in need of residential care, together with the 'casuals' – the tramps or 'persons without a settled way of living'. The committees ran children's homes, organised the fostering of children and provided non-institutional help such as 'medical relief' for the sick and 'out-relief' for other categories of need. From 1931 to 1934 they were also responsible for the assessment and payment of unemployment benefit.

Where to find the records
Public Assistance Committee minutes and the minutes of the Area Guardians Committees are at HALS (HALS: HCC 37). A name index of these volumes has been started.

Hospitals and asylums

Before the establishment of the National Health Service (NHS) Hertfordshire had an assortment of hospitals varying greatly in quality and size. Their records have not always survived but an entry in a register may provide unique evidence of an ancestor's physical or mental health. Medical records are subject to 100-year closure and all NHS records, as public records, are closed to public access for thirty years.

Engraving of Hertford County Hospital (then General Infirmary), Rock & Co. 1854 (Ref. County Views Hertf/13).

Isolation hospitals had existed from the eighteenth century in the form of 'pest houses' but it was only after the Isolation Hospitals Act of 1893 that county councils were empowered to provide hospitals for people suffering from infectious diseases such as smallpox, scarlet fever or diphtheria. *Voluntary hospitals* were privately endowed institutions for the 'deserving poor' and were maintained by subscriptions and donations. *Workhouse hospitals* had started life as infirmaries of the union workhouses run by the Boards of Guardians. Unlike the voluntary hospitals, workhouse hospitals were not permitted to turn patients away.

Asylums for the mentally ill were privately run under licences granted at Quarter Sessions. The Local Government Act of 1888 placed the responsibility for their provision upon the new county councils, which also took over the workhouse infirmaries in 1929. Hospitals maintained by local authorities were transferred to the Minister of Health in 1948 on the founding of the NHS.

Where to find the records

HALS holds records, varying in quantity, for a number of pre-NHS hospitals (HALS: HI, HV and HW), but amongst these there are few relating to patients and the majority tend to be post-1900. In-patient registers may give information such as: name, age, address, nature of illness, date of admission, date of discharge and occasionally patient's occupation. Records that may be of help to family historians include:

♦ Isolation hospitals: South Lodge Isolation Hospital, Baldock, admission register 1940-5 (HALS: HI 2/3A/1); Bennets End Isolation Hospital, Hemel Hempstead, register of in-patients 1929-48 (HALS: HI 5/3A); Sisters Isolation Hospital, St Albans, admission and discharge register 1893-1950 (HALS: Off Acc 1162); Tring Isolation Hospital, admission register 1934-48 (HALS: HI 11/3B/1)

♦ Voluntary hospitals: West Herts Hospital, Hemel Hempstead, various including in-patient registers 1893-1946, out-patient registers 1891-1947, register of military cases 1914-18, admission book 1936-7 (HALS: HV 2); North Herts and South Beds Hospital, Hitchin, in-patient register 1945-50 (HALS: HV 4/3A)

♦ Workhouse hospitals: St Paul's Hospital, Hemel Hempstead, patient registers 1935-48 (HALS: HW 1/3A/1-12), register of military cases 1939-46 (HALS: HW 1/3B/1); Wellhouse Hospital, Barnet, daybooks and patient registers 1941-6 (HALS: HSS 3/2/1-3)

A few administrative records relating to the early licensing of private asylums in the county are amongst the Quarter Sessions records; see also documents relating to 'lunacy' such as returns of lunatics and notice of admissions (HALS: QS Misc B/1-25).

At the beginning of the nineteenth century there was still no county asylum for Hertfordshire, but by 1837 provision had been made for pauper and criminal lunatics to be received in the Bedford County Asylum. By 1856 an asylum had been built jointly by Hertfordshire, Bedfordshire and Huntingdonshire. This was located in Stotfold, Bedfordshire, and was known as the Three Counties Asylum (later Fairfield Hospital). A few administrative records relating to Hertfordshire patients in the Bedford County and Three Counties lunatic asylums exist amongst the Quarter Sessions records (HALS: QS Misc B; QS Var). The main series of records relating to the Three Counties Asylum is held by the Bedfordshire and Luton Archives and Record Service.

In 1899 Hill End Hospital in St Albans was opened for Hertfordshire patients. The hospital is now closed and the main series of Hill End records is held at HALS under the reference: Off Acc 1025. These are quite extensive but 100-year closure restrictions on access apply to all casebooks and medical records. Records for Cell Barnes Hospital have also been deposited and similar restrictions apply.

It is worth noting that, because of the county's proximity to London, several asylums were built in the south of Hertfordshire in the early twentieth century to take patients from London and Middlesex. The majority of the relevant records for these hospitals are held by the London Metropolitan Archives: Leavesden Hospital (now closed); Harperbury Hospital; Shenley Hospital (now closed); Napsbury Hospital (now closed, also took some patients from south Hertfordshire). HALS does hold some administrative records for Napsbury and Shenley hospitals.

On a national basis, the Hospital Records Database is an internet project undertaken jointly between the Public Record Office and the Wellcome Trust. It is designed to be a searchable on-line database bringing together information on the existence and whereabouts of hospital records throughout the country. It includes administrative details of the hospitals and their status or type, the location and covering dates of administrative and clinical records, and the existence of lists, catalogues or other finding aids. It can be accessed at <http://hospitalrecords.pro.gov.uk/>.

Gypsies and travellers
It can be particularly difficult for family historians to trace itinerant ancestors who may not be recorded in the more common genealogical sources.

Gypsy encampment on Colney Heath in the 1920s (Ref. Local Studies collection).

Although some of these 'strollers', 'travellers', 'vagrants' and 'vagabonds' will be simply those who lived on the fringes of society, others may have been members of the Gypsy community with their own ethnic identity, culture and language. There were also people who travelled with their work, whether as navvies (labourers) on the roads, railways or canals, or simply as pedlars or itinerant traders.

Gypsy families, and many other travellers, generally followed the same circuit each year through a county or region, taking advantage of the business opportunities of pleasure/trading fairs and markets. So those who saw Hertfordshire as their 'home territory' also ventured into Bedfordshire, Buckinghamshire, Cambridgeshire and Essex. Nineteenth century trade directories can be useful here, pinpointing the times when such fairs and markets took place.

Hertfordshire Quarter Sessions calendars can be searched for terms such as Egyptians, Gypsies, vagrants and vagrancy, and for licences granted to hawkers as badgers and higglers (see Licensed Occupations, Chapter 4). A name list of vagrants' convictions and passes 1816-20 can be found in Volume IX of the published Quarter Sessions calendars. Poor law settlement examinations and certificates may also be helpful.

Most Gypsy children were baptised but often did not have their births registered and so the International Genealogical Index (IGI) is valuable for tracking a family's movements across the county using baptisms. This will also be useful for men in occupations whose families moved with them, e.g. navvies. Marriages in church were rare for Gypsies, who performed their own ceremonies, although there are exceptions in some Hertfordshire families, such as the Shaws and Brinkleys. Gypsy burials took place in parish churchyards and cemeteries and monuments were often erected; deaths were therefore usually registered. There may be comments recorded in parish registers if a traveller is buried, married or has his children baptised in a place that is not his home.

Census returns can help to 'fix' nomadic individuals at a particular place and time. In 1841 and 1851 enumerators were instructed to record people not living in houses by number rather than by name, but in 1861 those in tents, caravans, barns or the open air should be recorded at the end of each enumeration district under a heading 'Persons not in houses'. From 1871 onwards, they should be recorded where they are found, in sequence with house-dwellers. If you find your ancestor in one census, try looking at the same location in other years: it may have been a regular camping place.

HALS also holds material such as press cuttings, photographs and articles which may help to suggest likely places to search for more information.

Suggested further reading
Floate, S.S., *My ancestors were Gypsies,* Society of Genealogists, 1999

Chapter 7

Schools and education

Classroom at Faudel Phillips School, Hertford c1890 (Ref. Local Studies collection).

Classroom at Faudel Phillips School, Hertford c1890 (Ref. Local Studies collection).

School records can provide the family historian with a glimpse of their ancestor's childhood – the school attended, the teachers, the lessons taught, the holidays and the punishments. The majority of schools for which records have survived are those that were taken over by county councils in 1902, but their roots lie in the nineteenth century development of education for all children. Hertfordshire was also (and still is) home to a number of centuries-old independent schools which attracted pupils from all over the country and from abroad.

Local authority schools

School log books and admissions registers are good sources for a period of your ancestor's life about which there may otherwise be very little information. There are restrictions on access to log books and punishment books containing entries less than sixty years old, and other records with material less than thirty years old.

Many Hertfordshire schools now run by the county council can trace their origins back to charitable bequests of the sixteenth and seventeenth centuries; these were known as 'voluntary aided schools' at the beginning of the twentieth century.

The state did not concern itself with education until 1833. Before that many different kinds of schools had been set up, some by philanthropic people or bodies, others for profit. The standard of teaching was also very variable with almost no provision for training new teachers. In consequence, most children received a very poor education or none at all.

In the early nineteenth century, two religious societies were founded to provide a basic education very cheaply. They were the National Society for Promoting the Education of the Poor in the Principles of the Church of England (National Schools) and the British and Foreign School Society (British Schools), a mainly nonconformist body. References to these schools can often be found in Victorian trade directories. At Hitchin, the nineteenth-century British Schools have been restored and are open to the public (see Appendix VI, Useful Addresses). The government gave small grants to the two religious societies in 1833, gradually increasing the amounts as the years progressed, appointing inspectors in 1839 and implementing the pupil teacher system in 1846 which helped to increase the number of teachers available.

By 1861 the payment of state grants to schools had come to depend on the numbers of children who attended and who passed a yearly examination. There were still areas of the county where there was virtually no school provision and Forster's Education Act of 1870 allowed board schools to be set up. These were to be non-denominational, financed by fees, a local rate and government grants and controlled by locally elected school boards.

In 1876 elementary education was made compulsory, although children could leave school at ten years old if a sufficient standard had been reached. Education was made free of charge in 1891. In 1902 local control of education passed to county councils. The minimum school leaving age was raised to twelve in 1899, fourteen in 1918, fifteen in 1944 and sixteen in 1972.

School records

From 1863 log books were required to be kept if schools received a government grant. The books give the names of teaching staff at the time of the Inspector's yearly visit and sometimes mention pupils by name. In Hertfordshire most log books date from about 1870.

Date	Name	Std	Punishl	Comment
1900 Oct 20	Henry Wilmot	4	2	Talking & playing.
	G. Hatton	2	1	Talking.
Nov 1	Henry Wilmot	4	2	} inattention
	Walter Ogner	4	2	
	Ed Bennington	1	2	
6	C Bennington	2	2	inattention
12	Maurice Carter	2	2	talking
14	Maurice Carter	2	1	playing
20	Geo Hatton	2	1	
20	Ed Bennetton	1	2	} inattention
.	Willie Rolph	1	2	
21	Percy Angell	4	2	
	Ernest Sommes	5	2	talking while the master was out of the room with Board members
	Herbert Carter	5	2	
	Wm Humphrey	6	2	
	Ruth Graves	5	2	
	Nora Swain	5	2	
	Ruth Graves	5	1	
25	Ed Bennetton	1	1	

From the punishment book for Breachwood Green School, Kings Walden, 1900 (Ref. HEd1/118/7).

Most schools, of whatever kind, kept a register of pupils' admissions. These registers usually contain the pupil's name, address, date of birth and date of entry to the school. They sometimes mention previous schools attended, the reason for leaving that school and the father's name and occupation. Some schools have registers of evacuees who attended during the Second World War.

Punishments were sometimes recorded in log books but after 1901 separate punishment books were kept, usually giving name, offence and punishment. Occasionally, remarks were written about the family.

School magazines and year books have not always survived but they may give lists of pupils' examination results or the names of those belonging to school teams. School histories are often published to mark a special anniversary and these can provide very useful background information.

School Attendance Committees functioned from 1876 to 1903 when county councils took over their powers. They summoned parents whose children did not attend school. The minutes contain the names of parents and their children not attending. Sometimes the age of the child is given. A few other papers concerning school attendance may also have survived.

When in 1902 all voluntary and board schools were taken over by the county council, there was a proliferation of records amongst those of the council, including the establishment of an Education Committee (HALS: HCC 21), to add to the records from the schools themselves.

Where to find the records

Papers relating to schools which began as parish charity schools or National Society schools are usually found among parish records (HALS:DP). These can include log books and admission registers.

Documents relating to schools which are, or have been in the past, under the control of the county council are referenced under HEd1 and HEd2 at HALS. Log books will be found for many schools, mostly beginning from the 1870s or later, although a few are of earlier date. Bramfield school, for instance, has a log book dating from 1863 (HALS:HEd1/16/1). There are also a number of early admission registers but punishment books are found less frequently.

School magazines and year books, as well as school histories, will be found at HALS, and reference should be made to the subject indexes.

Copies may also be found in the reference or local studies sections of Hertfordshire libraries.

School Attendance Committee records are among Boards of Guardians papers at HALS, as are the few references to the education of workhouse children. Committee minutes survive for the following unions:

◆ Barnet Union 1892-1903 (HALS:BG/BAR 86)
◆ Bishop's Stortford Union 1877-1903 (HALS:BG/BIS 92)
◆ Buntingford Union 1877-1900 (HALS:BG/BUN 8-14)
◆ Cheshunt Union 1895-1903 (HALS: HEd 5/10/1)
◆ Hertford Union 1877-1903 (HALS:BG/HER 61)
◆ Hertford Borough 1880-1 (HALS: HB)
◆ Hitchin Union 1877-1903 (HALS:BG/HIT 178-179, 231)
◆ Ware Union 1877-96 (HALS:BG/WAR 102)

The records also include a list of all children not attending school in Hertford in 1877 (HALS: Acc 93), and for Bishop's Stortford a school attendance census register for 1893 (HALS:BG/BIS 169).

Staff records may also be found with those of the school, such as a teaching staff appointments register 1902-36 for Alleyne's Grammar School, Stevenage (HALS: HEd1/57), or a staff register 1887-1946 for the Queen Elizabeth Grammar School, Barnet (HALS: HEd1/8/15).

Further education and training colleges

The records deposited at HALS relating to colleges of further education (at St Albans, Watford and Hemel Hempstead) are currently restricted for access, as they are predominantly post-1950. The material is mostly administrative with few, if any, student or staff related documents. A similar situation applies with the teacher training colleges at Balls Park, Wall Hall, Offley and Gaddesden.

Hockerill Training College at Bishop's Stortford was established in 1852 by the Church of England for the training of women teachers. The records have been deposited at HALS and include student registers 1852-84 and 1937-57 (HALS: DE/Hk/2/12/1-3); Hockerill Old Students Association magazine 1896-1978 (HALS: DE/Hk/3/4) and a register of staff 1898-1934 (HALS: DE/Hk/2/11/4). There are also log books for the 'practising schools' where the students were trained 1863-1950 (HALS: DE/Hk/ 3/1/1-10).

Records of the Oaklands Institute of Agriculture at St Albans deposited at HALS include scholarship registers (indexed) 1904-39 (HALS: HEd16/8-10) and a register of appointments 1904-32 (HALS: HEd16/16).

Independent and other schools

Hertfordshire has been the home of a variety of non-state schools, some of them public boarding schools for fee-paying scholars, others with charitable origins which subsisted on private donations.

Many of the well-established schools have published yearbooks, histories, rolls of honour or student registers. A wide selection is held at HALS and some examples are mentioned below; printed works may also be found at main Hertfordshire libraries. In general, the records are held by the schools concerned, and researchers who believe that their ancestor attended an independent school should consult a current gazetteer such as the *Independent Schools Yearbook* to find out if it is still in existence and its current address. They include:

◆ Aldenham School, Elstree, Herts WD6 3AJ: founded in 1597. Several editions of their Register have been published to date, as well as a history of the school; see also Beevor, E., *Register of Aldenham School 1836-1897,* 1897.

◆ Berkhamsted Collegiate School, Castle Street, Berkhamsted, Herts HP4 2BB: founded in 1541 as a grammar school.

◆ The Haberdashers' Aske's School, Butterfly Lane, Elstree, Herts WD6 3AF: founded in 1690. Transferred from Hoxton to Hampstead in 1898, and in 1961 to Elstree.

◆ Haileybury, Hertford Heath, Herts SG13 7NU: originally the East India Company's training college, it closed in 1858 after the Indian Mutiny and reopened as a school in 1862. A list of all students 1806-57 is included in *Memorials of Old Haileybury College,* 1894. See also Farrington, A., *The Records of the East India College,* Haileybury 1806-1858, HMSO, 1976. *The Haileybury Register 1862-1931* is on the shelves at HALS.

◆ Merchant Taylors' School, Ashwell, Herts. See Baker, Revd W., *Merchant Taylors' School register 1871-1900,* 1907. Minutes and miscellaneous papers 1903-99 have been deposited (HALS: Acc 3642, 3749).

◆ St Albans School, Abbey Gateway, St Albans, Herts AL3 4HB: a monastic foundation from the tenth century which became a free school after the dissolution of the monasteries. Students who fought in the Boer War are commemorated in Ashdown, C., *The Old Albanian Roll of Honour 1899-1902,* 1904.

◆ St Edmund's College, Old Hall Green, Ware, Herts SG11 1DS: formed in 1793 from an amalgamation of Silkstead School and students from the Douai English College, the latter founded in 1568 in France to educate Catholic priests and laymen but forcibly closed during the French Revolution.

◆ Reed's School, Cobham, Surrey KT11 2ES: founded in 1813 and known as the London Orphan Asylum while based at Watford. See Alvey, N., *Education by election, Reed's School, Clapton and Watford,* Hertfordshire Architectural and Archaeological Society, 1990.

◆ The Royal Masonic School for Girls, Rickmansworth Park, Rickmansworth, Herts WD3 4HF: founded in 1788, moved to Rickmansworth in 1934.

- The Princess Helena College, Preston, Hitchin, Herts SG4 7RT: founded in 1820.
- St Margaret's School, Merry Hill Road, Bushey, Herts WD23 1DT: founded in 1749.

There were many more, some short-lived, private schools, and for most it is unlikely that records have survived at all. References may be found in local trade directories. Where schools have moved to or from other counties, there may be records in the relevant county record offices.

Suggested further reading
Chapman, C., *Basic facts about using education records*, FFHS, 1999
Chapman, C., *The growth of British education and its records*,
    Lochin Publishing, 1992

Chapter 8
Military ancestors

No standing army existed in England and Wales until the seventeenth century. Before that, armies were raised as required from the adult male population, called annually to muster for the militia. After the Civil War and subsequent restoration of the monarchy, from 1660 a small standing army was maintained by the state which, in times of foreign conflict, had to be reinforced from the local militia. Army reforms of the nineteenth century created the regimental structure that has persisted, although greatly reduced, to this day. The records have often not survived in any quantity over the period, but there are various sources available which will be useful tools for the family historian whose ancestor served in arms, from muster rolls of the sixteenth century to twentieth century records of the two world wars.

Lieutenant Bernard Croft of the Hertfordshire Militia (Ref. DE/Yo/1/53).

Early muster rolls
For the sixteenth and early seventeenth centuries, muster rolls (i.e. name lists of men called to serve in the militia) may be valuable sources for family historians, although their survival rate has not been good.

During the medieval period and until the mid-seventeenth century, armies were raised as required from the local militia. Every able-bodied man aged sixteen to sixty was liable for military service and a general muster was called annually to count men and arms available. Henry VIII required frequent musters to be held and returns of those attending were sent to the Secretary of State.

Where to find the records
A few muster rolls survive locally but the majority are held at the Public Record Office amongst the State Papers Domestic, the Exchequer Accounts and the Audit Office Accounts. These include muster rolls for Edwinstree

Example of a muster roll from 1808 (Ref. MIL9/53).

Hundred 1535 (PRO: E101); Hertford 1539 (PRO: SP1); St Albans 1573 (PRO: SP12); indenture rolls 1591-1601 (PRO: E101); the county 1635 (PRO: SP14) and indenture rolls 1626-7 and 1639 (PRO: SP16). A muster book for the hundreds of Cashio and Dacorum 1640 is held at the British Library (Harl. Mss. 2285).

The records held at HALS have usually survived amongst deposited private collections or parish records, including a muster book 1583-98 for the hundreds of Edwinstree and Odsey (HALS: 6990); a transcript by Cussans from the PRO State Papers Domestic of Hertfordshire horsemen mustered in 1583 (HALS: DE/Cu/1, p.142); a list of Aspenden men conscripted to the national militia 1651-75 (HALS: DP/8/8/1) and a list of finders of horse, officers and soldiers in the militia under the command of Sir John Bucknall, Hertford, 1690 (HALS: 79902).

Three muster books for the hundreds of Edwinstree and Odsey (with neighbouring parishes in the hundreds of Broadwater and Braughing) have been published: King, A., (ed) *Muster Books for North and East Hertfordshire 1580-1605,* Hertfordshire Record Society, 1996. These were transcribed from the archives of the Capel family (HALS: 6990, 8283, 9531).

Suggested further reading
Gibson, J. and Dell, A., *Tudor and Stuart Muster Rolls,* FFHS, 1991

Militia lists 1757-1801
Hertfordshire has a valuable genealogical source in its unusually comprehensive set of militia ballot lists. These name lists, which may also give occupations, infirmities and family details, are a unique pre-census source for discovering where in the county a family was located.

Militia lists are parish returns of those men between the ages of eighteen and fifty (from 1762, eighteen to forty-five) liable to serve in the county militia, which was re-established as a part-time, county-based force under the 1757 Militia Act. These returns, otherwise called militia ballot lists, are in effect a census of nearly the whole of the local adult male population.

A group of the Hertfordshire Militia (Ref. DE/Yo/1/53).

The returns were sent by the parish constable to the clerk of the court of Quarter Sessions, where balloting took place to decide who should serve in the militia. Men served initially for three years, later extended to five years, and were not called on to serve overseas, although they might be sent anywhere in Britain. It was possible to pay a substitute to take your place and to appeal against inclusion. Exemptions were granted to those men who had already served, were infirm or had a large number of dependents who would otherwise be a burden on the poor rates. Peers, clergymen, teachers, magistrates, apprentices, soldiers, seamen and constables were automatically exempt but may still be listed.

Where to find the records

From a militia list for Standon, 1762 (Ref. QS records).

The returns were made intermittently after 1757 and in Hertfordshire they survive for the following years: 1758-65; 1768-9; 1772-3; 1775; 1778; 1780-7; 1792-4; 1796-8; 1801. Most parishes have returns for the years 1758-80, while fewer have surviving records for the period after 1780. Returns for 1803-4 are contained in a militia book covering Hertford and Braughing hundreds. There is an alphabetical list of parishes (including dates of surviving militia lists) in the Quarter Sessions catalogue at HALS. Hertfordshire Family History Society have published indexed transcripts of the lists by parish, and the full series is available at HALS.

Related records include:

- rolls of men serving in the militia: Cashio Hundred 1760-2; Edwinstree and Odsey hundreds 1760-2; Dacorum Hundred 1760-62, 1765 (HALS: QS/MIL 9/5, 11, 12, 15). These are the final lists after balloting, on which the names of substitutes are entered and for whom each substitute served.
- *posse comitatus* lists 1798 for Essendon (HALS: DP/37/10/2); *levée en masse* lists 1803 for Hitchin (HALS: 66987). Lists of men who were eligible to form a reserve defence force, drawn up by the parish constables.
- muster rolls for the county 1759-61 (HALS: DE/P/F/269)

There are also associated militia records at the Public Record Office, including the County Regimental Returns for the Militia 1781-1876 (PRO: WO 13/988-1011); the Supplementary Militia 1799-1814 (PRO: WO 13/2510) and the Local Militia, East Midland and Western 1808-16 (PRO: WO 13/3504-6).

Volunteer and Territorial forces in Hertfordshire

While militia ballot lists form, for family historians, perhaps the most accessible records relating to this period in Hertfordshire, the militia was not the only local force which was formed in the eighteenth century. Volunteer and Territorial forces were in some cases shortlived, but in others they evolved into regiments which served in the two world wars of the twentieth century and beyond.

The records held locally for these forces are relatively few but an outline of the genealogy of the various corps and regiments is given below, to the eve of the Second World War. This is a necessarily brief summary and family historians who would like a more detailed account of their evolution will find Sainsbury, J., *Hertfordshire's Soldiers from 1757,* Hertfordshire Local History Council, 1969, and other works by this author, useful.

- Hertfordshire Militia: raised 1757 and embodied intermittently; 1881 became 4th Battalion, Bedfordshire Regiment (Herts Militia); demobilised 1919.
- Hertfordshire Volunteer units (local defence corps): raised 1794; 1808 many volunteers transferred to the new Hertfordshire Local Militia; by 1813 all such units had been disbanded.
- Hertfordshire Yeomanry and Volunteer Cavalry: several Troops raised in the county 1794-1831, most existing for only a short period. In 1870 the South Hertfordshire Troop became the Hertfordshire Yeomanry Cavalry, incorporating the Northern Troop in 1871. In 1901 this became the Hertfordshire Imperial Yeomanry; in 1908 the Hertfordshire Yeomanry. Demobilised in 1919, reformed 1920 and amalgamated with the 1st and 2nd Hertfordshire Batteries, 4th East Anglian Brigade, RFA (* below) as

(briefly) 3rd East Anglian Brigade, RFA, soon the 86th (East Anglian) (Hertfordshire Yeomanry) Brigade, RFA. Reclassified as a Regiment in 1938. Two cadres formed the 79th (Hertfordshire Yeomanry) Heavy Anti-Aircraft Regiment, RA 1938-45 and the 135th (East Anglian) (Hertfordshire Yeomanry) Field Regiment, RA, 1939-45.

◆ 1st Hertfordshire Light Horse Volunteers: 1862-79.
◆ 42nd (Hertfordshire) Company, Imperial Yeomanry: 1899-1901, raised from the Hertfordshire Yeomanry Cavalry, with additional volunteers.
◆ Hertfordshire Rifle Volunteers: raised 1859. In 1887 became the 1st and 2nd (Hertfordshire) Voluntary Battalion, Bedfordshire Regiment, and in 1908 was amalgamated into the 1st Battalion, Hertfordshire Regiment, plus formed 1st and 2nd Hertfordshire Batteries, 4th East Anglian Brigade, RFA (*). The 1st Battalion, Hertfordshire Regiment was demobilised 1919, reformed 1920.

The regimental collection of the Hertfordshire Regiment (Territorial Army) is held at Hertford Museum, Bull Plain, Hertford.

In 1919 the Bedfordshire and Hertfordshire Regiment was formed (regular army) from the Bedfordshire Regiment (originally the 16th Regiment of Foot) and its Hertfordshire components. In 1958 this amalgamated with the Essex Regiment to form the 3rd East Anglian Regiment. The regimental collection of the Bedfordshire and Hertfordshire Regiment is housed at Luton Museum, Wardown Park, Luton, Bedfordshire.

The other regular army regiment with a Hertfordshire connection was originally the 49th (Hertfordshire) Regiment of Foot, raised in 1744 and linked by name to the county in 1782. In 1816 it became known as Princess Charlotte of Wales's Own, and in 1881 was redesignated the 1st Battalion Princess Charlotte of Wales's (Berkshire) Regiment. The regimental museum of the Royal Berkshire Regiment is at Salisbury, Wiltshire.

Where to find the records

A limited quantity of military records have been deposited at HALS: DE/Yo is a collection of regimental and other papers relating to volunteer, territorial, auxiliary and reserve military units raised in Hertfordshire between 1663 and 1994; QS/MIL 9 includes records of the militia and volunteer corps. Family historians may find little that will be of direct genealogical help but regimental histories and other material can provide useful background information (see also below for First and Second World War service).

Of particular interest may be:

◆ Hertfordshire Militia (the 4th Battalion, Bedfordshire Regiment (Hertfordshire Militia) from 1881): names of officers 1764 (HALS: QS/MIL 9/13); lists of officers 1800-1914 (HALS: DE/Yo/1/2); photograph albums 1850s-1915 (HALS: DE/Yo/1/5, 51-53)

- 2nd (Hertfordshire) Volunteer Battalion, Bedfordshire Regiment (was 2nd Hertfordshire Rifle Volunteer Corps to 1887): muster book 1881-1908 (HALS: DE/Yo/1/7)
- Dacorum Troop of Hertfordshire Yeomanry Cavalry: attendance rolls April/May 1833 (HALS: DE/Yo/2/1)
- Hertford Volunteer Infantry: muster roll 1804 (HALS: DE/Hx/Z27)
- County Volunteer Corps: muster rolls 1808-22 (HALS: QS/MIL 9/51-146)
- Volunteer Corps: muster rolls extracts re Hertfordshire men serving in neighbouring County Volunteer Corps (chiefly Buckinghamshire, Essex and Middlesex) (HALS: QS/MIL 9/29-50)
- Hitchin Volunteer Corps 1798-1816: includes roll books and pay lists (see *Guide to the Hertfordshire Record Office,* page 215)
- HM Navy: parish return of persons enrolled to serve as volunteers for the Hundred of Broadwater 1795 (HALS: QS/MIL 9/18-28)

Military service in the British Army: First and Second World Wars
Many family historians will be tracing ancestors who served in the armed forces during the two world wars, not necessarily with a direct Hertfordshire connection.

The main sources for military ancestors during the twentieth century will be in the personal and regimental records held at the Public Record Office, but there is a range of useful publications and other material at HALS which will complement and may simplify research for family historians.

Soldiers died in the Great War: originally published in 81 volumes, arranged by regiment and battalion, this huge work is now available in a searchable form on CD-ROM at HALS. It gives regiment, rank, and service number, and limited information on next of kin and place of origin.

Volumes 2 (Royal Horse and Royal Field Artillery), 3 (Royal Garrison Artillery), 75 (Machine Gun Corps, Tank Corps), 77 (includes Hertfordshire Regiment), and 79 (Royal Army Medical Corps) are available in printed form on the open shelves (published by J.B. Hayward and Sons 1998/1999).

Soldiers died in the Second World War on CD-ROM is also available for searching at HALS.

Rolls of Honour (national): other published works at HALS which list men and women who died in the First and Second World Wars include:
- *The Cross of Sacrifice 1914-1919,* volumes 1-4: officers who died in the service of British, Commonwealth and Colonial navies, regiments and corps, and air forces
- *Airmen died in the Great War 1914-1918:* roll of honour of the British and Commonwealth Air Services, compiled by Chris Hobson

- *British Red Cross and Order of St John Enquiry List no. 14, 1917 Wounded and Missing,* first published 1917, reprinted 1989, Sunset Militaria
- *A register of Royal Marines deaths 1939-1945,* Royal Marines Historical Society, 1992
- *Roll of Honour, Land Forces World War Two,* volumes 1-4, edited by Joseph Devereux and Graham Sacker, Promenade Publications, 2000

Rolls of Honour (Hertfordshire): some parish rolls of honour were printed following each war, and a few examples of these are on the open shelves at HALS; copies may also be found at local libraries. Schools often also published rolls of honour naming past pupils who had died on active service. A diocesan roll of honour for Hertfordshire (First World War) is also available. Renewed interest in the subject over the past few years has led to local publications giving details of the men and women named on town and village war memorials.

Commonwealth War Graves Commission Debt of Honour Register: The Commonwealth War Graves Commission (CWGC) maintains the graves of nearly two million members of the Commonwealth forces who fell during the two world wars and beyond. The Debt of Honour Register provides personal and service information, sometimes quite detailed, on these men and women, including the regiment, battalion and company in which they served, the circumstances during which they fell, name of next of kin, place of origin and location of the cemetery in which they were buried or where they are commemorated. The CWGC also maintains a register of UK civilian casualties during the Second World War.

The Commission is located at 2 Marlow Road, Maidenhead, Berks. SL6 7DX and enquiries can be made by post (for a small charge). The index, however, can easily be searched online at <www.cwgc.org>.

Absent Voters' Register 1918: see Chapter 3. This electoral register can give useful information including rank, service number and regiment, for soldiers of voting age (nineteen years and over).

Army, Navy and Air Force Lists: These are annual published lists of those officers serving with the armed forces, including those in receipt of retired pay. HALS holds copies for the following periods, with some gaps:
- Army Lists – July 1842 (HALS: 16907), 1914, 1967 to date. Officers in receipt of retired pay 1968-98.
- Navy Lists – Containing lists of ships, establishments and officers of the fleet 1967 to date. Appendix containing rates of pay etc 1967-81. Retired officers 1967-95.
- Air Force Lists – 1967 to date. Retired list 1973-96.

Local newspapers: newspapers often printed news of local men and women, including reports of their death. Sometimes photographs are included. If the date of death is known (or of other newsworthy events, such as the award of medals) it is worth looking at editions of the newspaper for the weeks following.

Suggested further reading

Using Army Records, PRO Pocket Guides to Family History, PRO, 2000

Fowler, S. and Spencer, W., *Army Records for the Family Historian,* PRO, 1998

Fowler, S., Spencer, W. and Tamblin, S., *Army Service Records of the First World War,* PRO, 2nd ed. 1997

Watts, C.T. and M.J., *My ancestor was in the British Army: how can I find out more about him?* Society of Genealogists, 1995.

Chapter 9

Printed sources

It is always a good idea to find out what is already known and has been published about your family or the community in which they lived, as this may save hours of work or provide clues to a missing ancestor. There are many printed pedigrees, family histories, local and county histories, as well as contemporary printed sources such as directories and newspapers which can help not only to trace individuals or families, but also to provide background information about the places and the times in which our ancestors lived. A word of caution, though – not everything that appears in print is correct, and family historians should still use primary sources such as those covered in this book to confirm events, dates, etc.

Directories

Locating individuals in the decades before the census in 1841, and between census years after that, can be difficult, but directories may give valuable help. They can also be used to recreate the commercial background to life in a town or village, as farmers, craftsmen and tradesmen are listed in even the earliest publications, as are local 'worthies'.

Trade directories have a long history; the first known British collection of names and trades was published for London in the seventeenth century. They tended to appear only for major commercial towns until the late eighteenth century. The *Universal British Directory,* covering some Hertfordshire towns, appeared in parts between 1790 and 1798. In 1814 James Pigot began publishing what became the first series of national directories, and Hertfordshire was included from 1823. Francis Kelly's first directory appeared in 1845 for the 'Six Home Counties', including Hertfordshire, and *Kelly's Directories* have since become the best known of all, continuing to publish until past the middle of the twentieth century.

Directories produced before the Victorian period contain less information than their later counterparts but do list, in alphabetical order, the names and addresses (i.e. the street, in a town) of people in each trade. Later directories in the Victorian years and beyond tend to follow a common pattern. Usually each one covers the whole of a county. Each town or large village has its own entry, which gives brief details of the locality and history, together with information on the church and chapel, the school and other buildings, and commercial information such as market and fair days, and carrier and postal services (smaller villages were often included in the nearest town's entry). After this come the names of the 'principal' inhabitants or 'gentry' and then lists, under different occupations, of the professional, business and trades people of the locality. By the end of the nineteenth century, some larger towns have their own directories and these provide more detail as the residents are listed street by street as well as alphabetically.

It is important to remember that directories do not include everyone: employees such as domestic servants and labourers were not included, and anyone objecting to their name appearing (or failing to provide the information to the publishers) would also be left out of the book. Furthermore, by the time the directory was published, it could already be a year or more out of date.

Page from a Pigot & Co directory showing Hoddesdon 1826/27

Where to find directories

HALS and the main Hertfordshire libraries hold a number of county and local directories, as well as a few for other counties. The Guildhall Library and the Society of Genealogists' library in London also hold good collections. The following listing is of directories (original copies and modern reprints) held at HALS and available on the open shelves.

County directories, in earliest date order:
Universal British Directory (Hertfordshire extracts) 1791-8
Holden's Annual Directory (national) 1811
Pigot & Co Commercial Directory (Hertfordshire section) 1823, 1826, 1828, 1832, 1833, 1838, 1839
Pigot & Co Commercial Directory (London, Middlesex, Hertfordshire, Essex, Surrey, Sussex) 1823, 1826
Kelly's Directory (Hertfordshire) 1851, 1855, 1862, 1869, 1870, 1874, 1882, 1886, 1890, 1895, 1898, 1899, 1902, 1906, 1908, 1910, 1914, 1917, 1918, 1922, 1929, 1933, 1937

Craven & Co (Bedfordshire and Hertfordshire) 1854
Post Office Directory (Hertfordshire) 1859, 1867, 1878
Cassey Directory (Hertfordshire and Cambridgeshire) 1864
Post Office Directory (Essex) 1878
Post Office Directory (Middlesex) 1878, 1895, 1926
Kelly's Directory (Essex, Hertfordshire and Middlesex) 1890
Kelly's Directory (Essex) 1895, 1917, 1926, 1929, 1937
Post Office Directory (London) 1921
Kelly's Directory (Essex and Hertfordshire) 1926
Hertfordshire & Essex Trades Directory 1944, 1960, 1963, 1966, 1968,
    1969, 1971, 1972
Middlesex & Hertfordshire Trade Directory 1949, 1951, 1954
South Eastern Counties Trade Directory 1953, 1970
Bedfordshire & Hertfordshire Trade Directory 1974, 1975, 1981

Town directories, in place order:
Kelly's Directory (Barnet) 1935, 1939
Barnet & East Barnet Directory 1951, 1954, 1961, 1962, 1963,
    1965, 1966
Berkhamsted Directory 1970
Mardon Bros. Yearbook, Directory & Almanack (Bishop's Stortford
    and area) 1910
Boardman's Directory (Bishop's Stortford) 1948
Bishop's Stortford Directory 1952, 1963-80 (some years missing)
Bushey Directory 1980, 1982
Kelly's Directory (Harpenden) 1967-74 inclusive
Hemel Hempstead Almanack 1889, 1890, 1891, 1895, 1897, 1899,
    1901, 1902, 1903
Simson's Directory (Hertford and Ware) 1920, 1924, 1927
Kelly's Directory (Hertford) 1936, 1938, 1940, 1943, 1945, 1958
Hertford Trade Directory 1964
Letchworth Printers Directory (Hitchin) 1948
Hitchin Directory 1948, 1952, 1956, 1960, 1965, 1968
Letchworth & Baldock Directory 1953, 1962, 1968
Kelly's Directory (St Albans) 1900, 1901, 1903, 1906, 1907, 1923,
    1926, 1927, 1928, 1932, 1936, 1937, 1938, 1941, 1949, 1952,
    1954, 1956, 1958, 1960, 1962, 1964, 1966-75 inclusive
Herts Advertiser Year Book & Directory of St Albans 1922
St Albans Year Book & Directory 1932
Ware & District Almanack 1916
Kelly's Directory (Watford) 1926, 1927, 1929, 1931, 1932, 1934-8,
    1940, 1947, 1949, 1952, 1954, 1956, 1958, 1960, 1962, 1964,
    1966, 1967-74 inclusive
Peacock's Directory (Watford) 1905, 1914, 1917, 1923, 1929

Watford Trades Directory 1962, 1975, 1983
Welwyn Garden City Directory 1926, 1928-41, 1947, 1948, 1953,
    1959, 1960, 1969

Suggested further reading
Mills, D., *Rural community history from trade directories*, Local Population
    Studies, 2001
Norton, J.E., *A guide to the national and provincial directories of England
    and Wales, excluding London, published before 1856*, Royal Historical
    Society, 1984
Shaw, G. and Tipper, A., *British directories: a bibliography and guide
    to directories published in England and Wales 1850-1950 and Scotland
    1773-1952*, Leicester University Press, 1988

Newspapers
*Local newspapers can be a mine of information for family historians although,
unless there is an index of names available, using them can be time consuming
and there is no guarantee of finding anything relevant. From the later years of
the nineteenth century there is a greater chance that ancestors' names may be
mentioned, whether in a court report or the proceedings of a horticultural show
or cricket match.*

Advertisement
encouraging emigration
to Canada from the
Hertfordshire Mercury
dated 21 February
1903 (Ref. PC70)

The earliest Hertfordshire newspapers for which copies are available at
HALS date from the late eighteenth century. 'Local' newspapers at that
time tended to be county-wide and often combined several counties within
their distribution area, such as the *County Press* for Hertfordshire,
Bedfordshire, Buckinghamshire, Essex, Cambridgeshire and Middlesex.

They would have been purchased by the middle and upper classes and the subject matter of early newspapers reflects this. As literacy increased through the nineteenth century, and newspapers became cheaper to buy, individual towns began to produce their own. The content became broader and can include court reports, local celebrations, unusual happenings or accidents, sports results, births, marriages and deaths, local politics and reports of the meetings of committees such as the Boards of Guardians.

Where to find the records

HALS holds a wide range of newspapers, many available on microfilm, and a selection of these films is also held by some Hertfordshire libraries. A full list of titles and all copies held in Hertfordshire is on the HALS website <www.hertsdirect.org/hals>; this also includes 'Title Histories', indicating where the names of newspapers have changed.

The national repository for all newspapers is the British Library Newspaper Library, Colindale Avenue, London NW9 5HE, and it is possible that gaps in coverage can be filled with the material held there (<www.bl.uk/catalogues/newspapers.html>).

The Hertfordshire Newspaper Picture Index 1890-1930, at HALS, contains over 11,000 entries of names of people whose picture appeared during that period in the *Hertfordshire Mercury, Watford Observer* or *Herts Advertiser*. A database of material gathered from the *Hertfordshire Mercury* 1851-71, which has been name-indexed, is held by Matthew Sears, 250 Westfield, Harlow, Essex CM18 6AP (see his website 'Hertfordshire Gleanings' at <www.victorianlondoners.com>). A copy of the preliminary name index for this is held at HALS but further information can be obtained from Mr Sears for a fee.

As an indication of coverage in Hertfordshire, the following newspapers are included amongst those on film at HALS:

Borehamwood and Elstree Post 1949-86

County Chronicle 1816, 1818-32

County Press 1831-8, 1851-2, 1854-5

Hemel Hempstead Gazette 1869, 1877, 1879, 1885, 1887-1908, 1912 to date

Hertford Record 1886-8, 1890

Herts Advertiser & St Albans Times 1858 to date

Hertfordshire & Cambridgeshire Reporter & Royston Crow 1855-65, 1876 to date

Hertfordshire Express 1859-70

Hertfordshire Mercury 1772, 1775, 1825 to date

The Reformer 1834-43

West Hertfordshire & Watford Observer 1863 to date

The Times newspaper was founded in 1785 and, despite being a national publication, often carried provincial news, especially if it was particularly odd, scandalous or amusing. It is easy to find out if your ancestor was mentioned by name, as the newspaper is fully indexed. In Hertfordshire, copies of Palmer's Index on CD-ROM (covering 1790 to 1908) and the Official Index to The Times (1906-1990) are held at the Central Resources Library (New Barnfield, Travellers Lane, Hatfield, Herts AL10 8XG), which also has The Times on microfilm. The complete indexes are at the British Library Newspaper Library, Colindale.

It is worth remembering that newspaper circulation did not follow county boundaries, and news of 'border' parishes may be found in the newspapers of a neighbouring county. *The Newsplan Report for South East Newspapers,* British Library, 1996, is held at HALS and can be a useful guide to where to find copies of particular newspapers.

Suggested further reading
Collins, A., *Basic facts about using Colindale and other newspaper repositories,* FFHS, 2001
Gibson, J., *Local newspapers 1750-1920: a select location list,* FFHS, 2002
Thwaite, M.F., *Hertfordshire newspapers 1772-1955,* Hertfordshire Local History Council, 1956

Miscellaneous printed sources
There are many other sources of information on library shelves for family historians, from transcriptions of original records, pedigrees and family trees, to county and local histories, autobiographies, and histories of schools, hospitals, and other institutions. Many of these have already been mentioned in previous chapters but there are some volumes of more general use. The following works are all held at HALS but there will be copies of many of these in major Hertfordshire libraries (see the online library catalogue <www.hertsdirect.org/libraries> to find where these, and other books of interest, are held).

Genealogical research was once the province of the landed gentry, anxious to prove their lineage and right to bear arms. Printed pedigrees therefore exist from the time of the Heralds' Visitations in the sixteenth century, and are a feature of the county histories published in the nineteenth century. There is also a collection of printed and unpublished pedigrees and family histories in the library at HALS.

◆ *Visitations of Hertfordshire, 1572 and 1634* (volume 22 of the Harleian Society's publications, 1886): pedigrees of families claiming the right to bear arms, collected by the Heralds of the College of Arms.
◆ Berry, W., *Pedigrees of Hertfordshire Families,* c.1839
◆ Clutterbuck, R., *The History and Antiquities of Hertfordshire,* three volumes, 1815-27: contains a number of detailed pedigrees.

(Also on microfilm at HALS.)

- Cussans, J.E., *History of Hertfordshire,* three volumes, 1870-81: has useful transcripts of some monumental inscriptions and family trees. Cussans' own grangerised copy of his work, in thirteen volumes and containing much additional documentary material, is also at HALS (Ref. DE/Cu). A selection from the latter has been published: Deacon, A. and Walne, P. (ed), *"A professional Hertfordshire tramp", John Edwin Cussans, Historian of Hertfordshire,* Hertfordshire Record Society, 1987
- Page, W. (ed), *The Victoria History of the County of Hertfordshire,* four volumes and index, 1902-3. This is excellent, particularly on manorial descents.
- Warrand, D. (ed), *Hertfordshire Families,* 1907: genealogical volume of the *Victoria County History,* an exhaustive and scholarly treatment of the pedigrees of twelve landed Hertfordshire families. (Also on microfilm at HALS.)

Transcriptions of original documents can be of great help and the following works, which have been referred to in earlier chapters, are name-indexed:
- Brigg, W., *Hertfordshire Genealogist and Antiquary,* three volumes, 1895-8. These volumes contain transcripts of the following:
  - marriage licences: Archdeaconry of St Albans 1583-1715; Archdeaconry of Huntingdon (Hitchin registry) 1610-49
  - abstracts of wills: Archdeaconry of Middlesex 1565-90; Archdeaconry of St Albans 1415-51; Archdeaconry of Huntingdon 1579-1601; Consistory Court of the Bishop of London 1586-1628
  - feet of fines for Hertfordshire 1485-1603
  - subsidy rolls for Hertfordshire 1545, and 1566-67 (Dacorum)
  - lists of Hertfordshire inquisitions post mortem, Henry VII to Charles I (names and dates)
  - transcripts from some early parish registers and bishops' transcripts for Bushey, Caldecote, Lilley, Newnham, Northaw, Redbourn, Rickmansworth, St Michael's, St Stephen's, Wigginton
  - genealogical miscellanea relating to Hertfordshire.
- Le Hardy, W., *Hertford Quarter Sessions Rolls and Books,* ten volumes, 1905-57. These volumes cover 1589-1894 (sessions rolls) and 1619-1843 (sessions books) respectively, fully indexed, and with a number of transcriptions of lists of licences, sacrament certificate holders and dissenters; *Sessions Records of the Liberty of St Albans Divison 1770-1840* forms Volume IV.
- Dean, D. (ed), *St Albans Quarter Sessions Rolls 1784-1820,* Hertfordshire Record Society, 1991

Other major sources include:

◆ Le Hardy, W., *Guide to the Hertfordshire Record Office Part 1: Quarter Sessions and other records in the custody of the officials of the county,* Hertfordshire County Council, 1961. Although now out of date, this contains useful background information on a wide range of sources.

◆ *The Gentleman's Magazine,* 1731-1866. This journal contains notices of births, marriages and deaths, obituaries and general news of business and professional families and the gentry. Entries relating to Hertfordshire have been extracted and published: Jones, A. (ed), *Hertfordshire 1731-1800 as recorded in the Gentleman's Magazine,* Hertfordshire Publications, 1993.

◆ *Dictionary of National Biography,* and twentieth century supplements

◆ Burke's *Peerage* (four volumes, 1839-1959), *Landed Gentry* (five volumes, 1886-1965), *Extinct Peerages* (1883) and *Extinct Baronetcies* (1838)

◆ Walford's *County Families,* two volumes, 1885 and 1906

◆ Cokayne, G.E., *Complete Peerage,* eight volumes, 1887-98, and *Complete Baronetage,* six volumes, 1900-6

◆ Humphery-Smith, C.R., *Armigerous ancestors,* Family History Books, 1997. A catalogue of sources for the study of the Visitations of the Heralds in the sixteenth and seventeenth centuries with referenced lists of names.

◆ Emden, A.B., *Biographical Registers* of Oxford and Cambridge Universities before 1500, four volumes, 1957-63

◆ Foster, J., *Alumni Oxonienses,* 1500-1886, eight volumes, 1891

◆ Venn, J. and J.A., *Alumni Cantabrigienses,* 1500-1900, ten volumes, 1922-54.

Appendix I

Parish list

The following list is intended to give an indication of the availability at HALS of parish registers, bishops' transcripts (BTs), modern transcriptions or indexes, hearth tax and land tax returns for Hertfordshire parishes. Gaps in coverage of more than ten years have been shown, though there may be other instances where the records for several years are missing from the sequence; full details are to be found in the catalogues at HALS.

There are a number of published and manuscript transcripts and indexes for parish registers held at HALS. As all marriage entries have been included in the Hertfordshire Marriage Index, marriage register and marriage BT transcripts have not been included in this listing. An indication is given of whether the transcripts/indexes are solely for bishops' transcripts (BT), baptismal records (C) or burial records (B).

Hearth tax returns held at the Public Record Office for 1662-3 (and in some parishes, for other years in the 1660s/1670s) have been microfilmed; the parishes for which returns are available at HALS are indicated by √ in the listing below. Land tax returns are also available on microfilm, as below.

Parish	Ref (HALS)	Baptism	Marriage	Burial	BTs	Banns	Transc	Hearth	Land
Abbots Langley	DP/63	1538-1653, 1680-1957	1538-1653, 1680-1988	1538-1653, 1678-1994	1570-1867	1754-1821, 1865-1990	1570-1800	√	1753-1825
[Abbots Langley: see also Bedmond and Langleybury]									
Albury	DP/1	1558-1995	1558-1998	1558-1995	1813-1865	1754-1812, 1823-1962	-	√	1753-1832
Aldbury	DP/2	1694-1968	1694-1968	1694-1934	1604-1618, 1695-1869	1804-1986	-	√	1753-1830
Aldenham *[Aldenham: see also Radlett]*	DP/3	1559-1964	1559-1968	1559-1679, 1713-1943	1604-1869	1754-1975	1559-1812	√	1753-1829
Amwell, Great	DP/4	1558-1986	1558-1993	1558-1928	1800-1869	1754-1979	1600-1657	√	1728-1831, 1863-1891
Amwell, Little (1864)	DP/48A	1864-1981	1865-1992	1864-1988	1865-1869, 1882	1864-1980	-	√	1712-1831, 1863-1891
Anstey	DP/5	1543-1857	1541-1836	1540-1923	1800-1840	1754-1797, 1824-1881	1540-1837	√	1746-1832
Apsley End (1872)	DP/47C	1871-1919	1872-1913	1871-1941	-	1872-1926	-	-	-
Ardeley	DP/6	1546-1880	1546-1837	1546-1872	1604-1869	1754-1808, 1823-1987	-	√	1746-1832
Arkley (1905)	DP/15A	1905-1964	1905-1985	-	-	1905-1989	-	-	-
Ashwell	DP/7	1686-1968	1686-1975	1678-1937	1604-1883	1754-1887, 1907-1989	1604-1863	√	1746-1832
Aspenden	DP/8	1559-1947	1559-2000	1559-1888	1604-1868	1754-1812, 1823-1935	1559-1836	√	1746-1832
Aston	DP/9	1559-1986	1558-1980	1558-1902	1604-1868	1754-1814, 1824-1866	-	√	1715-1831, 1863-1891
Ayot St Lawrence	DP/10	1566-1999	1583-1996	1580-1998	1604-1869	1767-1803	-	√	1715-1831, 1863-1891
Ayot St Peter	DP/11	1687-1896	1686-1988	1686-1986	1604-1869	1773-1812, 1824-1979	-	√	1715-1831, 1863-1891
Baldock	DP/12	1558-1967	1558-1961	1558-1908	1604-1872	1754-1779, 1797-1813, 1880-1937	-	√	1715-1831, 1863-1891
Barkway	DP/13	1539-1967	1539-1984	1539-1916	1800-1835	1754-1813, 1823-1840, 1880-1947	1781-1856, 1915-1939	√	1754-1832

| Parish | Ref (HALS) | PARISH REGISTERS | | | | | | TAX | |
		Baptism	Marriage	Burial	BTs	Banns	Transc	Hearth	Land
Barley	DP/14	1559-1988	1560-1988	1559-1988	1802-1849	1754-1814, 1859-1988	1559-1812	√	1746-1825
Barnet, Chipping	DP/15	1603-1984	1560-1979	1592-1891	1563-1848	1755-1812, 1823-1976	1569-1795 BT	√	1753-1825,
St Stephen	DP/15	1945-1967	1923-1988	-	-	-	-	-	-
[Barnet: see also Arkley and Lyonsdown]									
Barnet, East	DP/16	1553-1963	1553-1973	1553-1934	1565-1869	-	1582-1793 BT	√	1753-1825
Barnet, New	DP/15C	1901-1957	1911-1974	-	-	1911-1979	-	-	-
Bayford (1867)	DP/37A	1538-1978	1538-1842	1538-1903	1604-1869	1856-1950	1538-1713	√	1715-1831, 1863-1891
Bedmond	DP/63	1950-1972	-	-	-	-	-	-	-
Bengeo									
St Leonard	DP/17	1539-1970	1539-1992	1547-1972	1604-1869	1754-1907, 1933-1995	1544-1994 B, 1539-1883 C	√	1714-1831, 1863-1891
St Mary		1962-1996	-	-	-	-	-	-	-
Christ Church (1869)	DP/17A	1869-1967	1869-1968	-	-	1935-1963	-	-	-
[Bengeo: see also Waterford]									
Benington	DP/18	1538-1961	1538-1980	1538-1882	1609-1869	1754-1823, 1866-1929	-	√	1715-1831, 1863-1891
Berkhamsted	DP/19	1538-1954	1538-1981	1538-1943	1604-1869	1754-1936, 1955-1991	-	√	1715-1830
[Berkhamsted: see also Potten End]									
Berkhamsted, Little	DP/20	1647-1900	1647-1901	1647-1915	1604-1868, 1881-1882	1756-1813, 1824-1913	-	√	1716-1831, 1863-1891
Bishop's Stortford									
St Michael	DP/21	1561-1991	1561-1995	1561-1913, 1961-1979	1800-1869	1754-1951, 1964-1984	1561-1712	√	1712-1831
Holy Trinity (1859)	DP/21A	1859-1985	1860-1978	-	1867-1869	1934-1975	1867-1869 C	-	-
[Bishop's Stortford: see also Hockerill]									
Borehamwood									
All Saints (1909)	DP/36A	1909-1965	1909-1964	-	-	1909-1990	-	-	-
Holy Cross		-	1969-1983	-	-	-	-	-	-
St Michael		1953-1967	1958-1989	-	-	1958-1988	-	-	-
Bourne End (1915)	DP/74A	1855-1908	1858-1947	1858-1915	1860-1877	-	-	-	-

		PARISH REGISTERS						TAX	
Parish	Ref (HALS)	Baptism	Marriage	Burial	BTs	Banns	Transc	Hearth	Land
Bovingdon	DP/47A	1675-1967	1674-2002	1674-1965	1604-1872	1861-1972	1604-1674 BT 1813-1905 B	√	1746-1830
Boxmoor (1829)	DP/47D	1830-1961	1844-1969	1832-1943	1843	-	-	-	-
Bramfield	DP/22	1560-1958	1559-1989	1560-1980	1604-1869	1755-1957	-	-	1753-1825, 1858-1890
Braughing	DP/23	1563-1925	1565-1971	1565-1881	1800-1846	1761-1765, 1779-1812, 823-1886	1563-1837	√	1714-1831
Bricket Wood (1981)	DP/94B	1937-1990	1974-1996	-	-	-	-	-	-
Broxbourne	DP/24	1688-1851	1688-1949	1688-1906	1800-1866	1754-1837, 1941-1983	-	√	1712-1831, 1863-1891
[Broxbourne: see also Hoddesdon and Rye Park]									
Buckland	DP/25	1658-1976	1662-1972	1662-1898	1801-1850	1754-1926	1658-1837	√	1746-1832
[Buntingford: see Layston]									
Bushey	DP/26	1684-1930	1684-1970	1737-1941	1560-1824	1844-1895, 1931-1991	1581-1800 BT	√	1746-1830
Bushey Heath (1889)	DP/26A	1888-1965	1889-1975	-	-	1960-1985	1888-1900 C	-	-
Bygrave	DP/27	1802-1980	1765-1964	1805-1980	1614-1869	1765-1808, 1824-1966	-	√	1746-1832
[earlier registers destroyed by fire]									
Caldecote	DP/28	1726-1970	1726-1974	1726-1964	1605-1869, 1882	1726-1802, 1944-1965	1610-1834	√	1746-1832
Chandlers Cross	DP/64A	-	-	-	-	-	-	-	-
Cheshunt St Mary	DP/29	1559-1995	1559-1995	1559-1981	1800-1866	1754-1852, 1948-1991	-	√	1712-1830, 1863-1891
Little St Mary	DP/29	1966-1975	-	-	-	-	-	-	-
[Cheshunt: see also Goffs Oak, Turnford and Waltham Cross]									
Chipperfield (1863)	DP/64A	1838-1973	1842-1989	1839-1962	1838-1865	1842-1967	-	-	-
Chorleywood Christ Church (1845)	DP/85A	1845-1990	1846-1979	1845-1938	-	1868-1990	-	-	-
St Andrew (1963)	DP/85E	1963-1986	1964-1975	-	-	1964-1987	-	-	-
Clothall	DP/30	1717-1904	1717-1989	1717-1990	1604-1869	1754-1812, 1915-1960	-	√	1746-1832
Codicote	DP/31	1559-1947	1559-1970	1559-1961	1560-1868	1753-1808, 1937-1959	1559-1867	√	1753-1825
Colney Heath (1846)	DP/93A	1847-1943	1847-1986	1846-1911	1848-1882	-	-	-	-

Parish	Ref (HALS)	PARISH REGISTERS						TAX	
		Baptism	Marriage	Burial	BTs	Banns	Transc	Hearth	Land
Cottered with Broadfield	DP/32	1563-1971	1558-1974	1558-1920	1604-1869	1779-1864, 1879-1977	-	√	1746-1832
Croxley Green									
All Saints (1872)	DP/85D	1872-1973	1873-1989	-	1872-1879	-	1872-1900 C	-	-
St Oswald	DP/85F	1937-1965	1946-1966	-	-	1946-1966		-	-
[Cuffley: see Northaw]									
Datchworth	DP/33	1570-1976	1570-1990	1570-1783, 1813-1953	1604-1869	1754-1812, 1824-1924	-	√	1715-1831, 1863-1891
Digswell	DP/34	1538-1989	1575-1992	1575-1993	1604-1866	1758-1812, 1823-1969	-	√	1715-1831, 1864-1891
Eastwick	DP/35	1555-1879	1556-1977	1555-1930	1800-1866	1755-1824	-	√	1714-1831
Elstree	DP/36	1656-1969	1656-1991	1656-1927	1575-1848	1755-1860, 1897-1908, 1965-1990	1655-1851	√	1753-1825
Essendon St Mary	DP/37	1653-1941	1653-1970	1653-1947	1604-1869	-	1635-1812	√	1711-1831, 1863-1891
Woodhill, St Mark	DP/37	1855-1975	1927-1975	1855-1902	1855-1869	1907-1975	-	-	-
[Essendon: see also Bayford]									
Flamstead	DP/38	1548-1892	1548-1929	1548-1902	1604-1874	1754-1806, 1824-1936	1548-1838	√	1798-1830
[Flamstead: see also Markyate]									
Flaunden	DP/47B	1729-1766, 1777-1949*	1729-1766, 1777-1948*	1729-1766, 1777-1812, 1834-1949*	1604-1867	-	-	√	1753-1830
		*[*microfilm only, original registers at Buckinghamshire Record Office]*							
Frogmore (1859)	DP/94A	1859-1949	1860-1971	1891-1943	1859-1860	1860-1970	-	-	-
Gaddesden, Great	DP/39	1559-1711, 1741-1948	1559-1689, 1741-1959	1558-1711, 1741-1917	1604-1883	1807-1970	1558-1840	√	1753-1830
Gaddesden, Little	DP/40	1681-1901*	1681-1901*	1681-1901*	1604-1863	1810-1818	-	√	1753-1830
		*[*microfilm only, original registers not held]*							
Gilston	DP/41	1558-1896	1559-1950	1558-1993	1800-1840	1754-1838	-	√	1711-1831
Goffs Oak (1871)	DP/29A	1868-1992	1871-1990	-	-	1871-1992	-	-	-
Graveley with Chivesfield	DP/42	1555-1974	1556-1961	1555-1946	1604-1868	1754-1792, 1824-1913	-	√	1715-1831, 1863-1891

Parish	Ref (HALS)	Baptism	Marriage	Burial	BTs	Banns	Transc	Hearth	Land
Hadham, Little	DP/43	1559-1910	1559-1994	1559-1930	1802-1868	1754-1812, 1896-1986	1559-1812	√	1746-1832
Hadham, Much	DP/44	1559-1908	1559-1986	1559-1928	1800-1867	1754-1807	-	√	1746-1831
Harpenden									
St Nicholas	DP/122A	1563-1961	1562-1961	1562-1938	1604-1866	1754-1768, 1823-1972	1562-1812 B, 1871-1891 C	√	1753-1830
St John (1937)	DP/122B	1926-1995	1932-1992	-	-	-	-	-	-
Hatfield	DP/46	1653-1922*	1654-1918*	1653-1940*	1604-1875	1754-1782	1653-1717	√	1715-1831, 1863-1891

[*microfilm only: original registers not held]

[Hatfield: see also Lemsford, Totteridge and Welwyn Garden City]

Parish	Ref (HALS)	Baptism	Marriage	Burial	BTs	Banns	Transc	Hearth	Land
Hemel Hempstead									
St Mary	DP/47	1558-1969	1558-1975	1558-1944	1604-1869	1754-1812, 1823-1978	-	√	1746-1830
St Paul (1878)	DP/47	1878-1945	1897-1988	-	-	1878-1930, 1962-1988	-	-	-
St Alban, Warners End	DP/47	1953-1982	1959-1996	-	-	1959-1990	-	-	-
St Barnabas	DP/47	1951-1980	1961-1981	-	-	1961-1981	-	-	-
St Peter, Gadebridge	DP/47	1958-1970	-	-	-	-	-	-	-
St Stephen	DP/47	-	-	-	-	1961-1972	-	-	-
All Saints, Picotts End	DP/47	-	-	-	-	-	-	-	-

[Hemel Hempstead: see also Apsley End, Bovingdon, Flaunden and Leverstock Green]

Parish	Ref (HALS)	Baptism	Marriage	Burial	BTs	Banns	Transc	Hearth	Land
Hertford									
All Saints & St John	DP/48	1559-1675, 1730-1975	1559-1675, 1730-1973	1559-1697, 1730-1951	1604-1869	1911-1995	1559-1779, 1559-1917	√	1713-1831, 1863-1891
St Andrew	DP/49	1560-1988	1561-1983	1561-1954	1604-1867	1760-1883, 1924-1982	1561-1900	√	1714-1831, 1863-1891
Hertingfordbury									
St Mary	DP/50	1679-1940	1679-1967	1679-1927	1604-1869	1763-1807, 1886-1978	-	√	1716-1831, 1863-1891
St John, Letty Green	DP/50	1883-1940	-	-	-	-	-	-	-
Hexton	DP/51	1538-1927	1539-1990	1538-1906	1575-1842, 1852-1868	1756-1802	1583-1797 BT	√	1753-1820
High Cross (1845)	DP/101A	1846-1924	1847-1985	-	1846-1858	1847-1913	-	-	-
High Wych (1862)	DP/98A	1861-1952	1862-1967	1861-1948	1861-1878	1913-1957	-	-	-
Hinxworth	DP/52	1558-1985	1558-1994	1558-1960	1605-1869	1754-1985	-	√	1746-1832

| Parish | Ref (HALS) | PARISH REGISTERS | | | | | | TAX | |
		Baptism	Marriage	Burial	BTs	Banns	Transc	Hearth	Land
Hitchin									
St Mary	DP/53	1562-1970	1562-1998	1562-1911	1604-1850	1754-1865, 1925-1987	1609-1641 C	√	1753-1830
St Mark	DP/53	1940-1995	-	-	-	-	-	-	-
St John	DP/53	1911-1947	-	-	-	-	-	-	-
Holy Saviour (1865)	DP/53A	1865-1979	1866-1966	1936-1993	-	-	-	-	-
St Faith	DP/53B	-	1967-1987	-	-	1967-1993	-	-	-
Hockerill All Saints (1852)	DP/21B	1852-1977	1852-1987	-	1852-1869	1896-1958, 1964-1990	-	-	-
Hoddesdon (1844)	DP/24A	1841-1949	1844-1949	1844-1870	1843-1866	1844-1989	-	√	1712-1831, 1863-1891
[Hoddesdon: see also Broxbourne and Rye Park]									
Holwell	DP/54	1560-1939	1560-1752, 1770-1992	1560-1812	-	1824-1990	-	-	-
Hormead, Great	DP/55	1538-1981	1538-1988	1538-1872	1800-1835, 1849-1852	1754-1812, 1823-1891	1538-1916	√	1746-1832
Hormead, Little	DP/56	1588-1886	1588-1886	1588-1994	1800-1802, 1813-1835, 1849-1850	1826-1950	1588-1916	√	1746-1832
Hunsdon	DP/57	1546-1931	1546-1986	1546-1890	1800-1838, 1860	1754-1772, 1847-1990	1546-1837	√	1715-1832
Ickleford	DP/58	1749-1933	1749-1988	1749-1877	1604-1868	1832-1958	1749-1812	√	1753-1830
Ippollitts	DP/59	1625-1977	1625-1972, 1981-1993	1625-1943	1604-1869	1754-1879	-	√	1753-1830
Kelshall	DP/60	1538-1916	1538-1985	1538-1987	1604-1869	1754-1932	-	√	1746-1832
Kensworth	*[Parish registers held at Bedfordshire and Luton Archives]* -								
Kimpton	DP/61	1559-1975	1568-1993	1564-1899	1604-1869	1754-1812, 1824-1946	1773-1812 C	√	1753-1830
Kings Langley	DP/64	1558-1978	1558-1995	1558-1970	1604-1869	1754-1817, 1891-1976	1558-1922	√	1753-1830
[Kings Langley: see also Chipperfield]									
King's Walden	DP/112	1558-1957	1558-1985	1558-1951	1604-1855	1754-1787, 1842-1920	1558-1721	√	1752-1830
[King's Walden: see also Preston]									
Knebworth									
St Mary	DP/62	1596-1946	1596-1951	1596-1950	1604-1868	1754-1812, 1846-1988	1596-1837	√	1724-1831, 1863-1891
St Martin	DP/62	1916-1959	1916-1990	1916-1974	-	1916-1979	-	-	-

			PARISH REGISTERS					TAX	
Parish	Ref (HALS)	Baptism	Marriage	Burial	BTs	Banns	Transc	Hearth	Land
Langleybury (1878)	DP/63A	1864-1971	1865-1965	1885-1961	1882	1977-1985	1864-1900 C	-	-
Layston with Buntingford	DP/65	1563-1931	1563-1996	1564-1971	1806-1852	1754-1812, 1823-1980	1563-1839	√	1746-1832
Leavesden (1853)	DP/117G	1853-1975	1854-1987	1853-1921	1854-1869, 1887	1941-1988	-	-	1753-1825
Lemsford (1858)		[no parish registers held]			1859-1868	-	-	-	-
Letchworth									
St Mary	DP/66	1695-1963	1695-1985	1695-1957	1604-1869	1754-1805	-	√	1715-1831, 1863-1891
St Michael All Angels	DP/66	-	1947-1973	-	-	-	-	-	-
St Paul (1963)	DP/66A	1930-1963	1957-1981	1963-1981	-	1957-1985	-	-	-
[Letty Green see Hertingfordbury]									
Leverstock Green (1850)	DP/47E	1849-1960	1850-1983	1850-1972	1852-1870	1971-1983	-	-	- -
Lilley	DP/67	1711-1895	1711-1985	1711-1897	1604-1869	1754-1814, 1824-1933	1609-1712	√	1753-1830
London Colney (1826)	DP/93B	1826-1964	1838-1992	1828-1958	1827-1852	1937-1981	-	-	-
Long Marston (1979)	DP/111A	1820-1871	1869-1993	1820-1978	1604-1882	1869-1947	-	-	1753-1830
Lyonsdown (1869)	DP/15B	1866-1892	1869-1911	-	1866-1876	-	-	-	-
Markyate (1877)	DP/38A	1855-1926	1879-1968	-	-	1878-1972	-	√	-
Meesden	DP/68	1737-1810	1738-1753, 1813-1837	1738-1810	1800-1840	-	-	√	1746-1832
Mill End with Heronsgate (1875)	DP/85C	1875-1974	1876-1991	-	-	1972-1978	1875-1900 C	-	-
Mimms, North	DP/69	1565-1567, 1663-1980	1663-1998	1663-1984	1604-1882	1754-1812, 1976-1996	1663-1812 B	√	1753-1830
Mimms, South									
K. Charles Martyr	DP/131	1938-1986	1941-1973	-	-	-	-	-	-
Christ Church	DP/133	1845-1968*	1854-1969*	-	-	-	-	-	-
St Giles	DP/132	1558-1856*	1558-1906*	1558-1898*					
[*microfilm only, original registers held at London Metropolitan Archives]									
Munden, Great	DP/70	1588-1988	1588-1983	1588-1939	1604-1868	1754-1776	-	√	1715-1832, 1863-1891
Munden, Little	DP/71	1680-1989	1680-1982	1680-1980	1604-1865	1754-1769, 1823-1975	1680-1812	√	1715-1832, 1863-1891
Nettleden	DP/39A	1813-1944	1833-1907	1813-1993	1845-1871	-	1687-1944	-	-

| Parish | Ref (HALS) | PARISH REGISTERS | | | | | | TAX | |
		Baptism	Marriage	Burial	BTs	Banns	Transc	Hearth	Land
Newnham	DP/72	1676-1982	1676-1987	1676-1983	1574-1854	1755-1792, 1816-1960	1676-1837, 1581-1799 BT	✓	1786-1825
Northaw St Thomas	DP/73	1571-1933	1571-1940	1571-1781, 1881-1964	1563-1869	1758-1990	1564-1793 BT, 1769-1812 C	✓	1735-1825
St Andrew, Cuffley	DP/73	-	1966-1975	-	-	-		-	-
Northchurch	DP/74	1564-1899	1621-1903	1564-1886	1604-1877	1754-1765, 1850-1918	-	✓	1705, 1753, 1780-1830
[Northchurch: see also Bourne End and Sunnyside]									
Norton St Nicholas	DP/75	1579-1985	1581-1989	1582-1974	1577-1869	1755-1812, 1823-1971	1579-1950	✓	1753-1825
St George	DP/75	-	1964-1974	-	-	1964-1985	-	-	-
St Thomas Becket	DP/75	1942-1954	1968-1974	-	-	1968-1984	-	-	-
Offley	DP/76	1653-1951	1654-1987	1653-1987	1604-1864	1754-1812, 1823-1962	-	✓	1753-1830
Oxhey St Matthew (1879)	DP/117F	1880-1963	1881-1977	-		1903-1991	1880-1900 C	-	
All Saints (1961)	DP/117J	1950-1982	1954-1986	-		1951-1985	-	-	
Chapel	DP/117F	1918-1948	1917-1975	-		-	-	-	
St Francis	DP/117F	-	1943-1968	-		1943-1969	-	-	
Pelham, Brent	DP/77	1539-1932	1551-1836	1539-1812	1829-1830	1653-1657, 1755-1810	1538-1855	✓	1746-1832
Pelham, Furneux	DP/78	1561-1990	1561-1992	1561-1991	1829-1831	1754-1812, 1824-1990	-	✓	1746-1832
Pelham, Stocking	DP/79	1695-1991	1695-1992	1695-1991	1805-1852	1754-1812	-	✓	1746-1832
Pirton	DP/80	1562-1908	1560-1991	1558-1995	1604-1869	1754-1970	-	✓	1753-1830
Ponsbourne	DP/37B	1863-1901	1878-1901	-	1863-1879	1878-1991	-	-	-
Potten End (1895)	DP/19A	1868-1936	1895-1912	1868-1985	-		-	-	-
Potters Bar	DP/130	1835-1961	1840-1929	1835-1933	-		-	-	-
Preston	DP/112	-	1909-1985	1900-1911	-		-	-	1753-1830
Puttenham	DP/81	1681-1812	1681-1993	1678-1992	1694-1869	1824-1964	-	✓	1746-1830
Radlett (1865)	DP/3A	1864-1964	1866-1974	1887-1943	1864	1866-1912, 1939-1989	-	-	-

| | | PARISH REGISTERS | | | | | | TAX | |
Parish	Ref (HALS)	Baptism	Marriage	Burial	BTs	Banns	Transc	Hearth	Land
Radwell	DP/82	1590-1989	1602-1963	1595-1982	1608-1868	1754-1812, 1839-1976	-	√	1754-1831
Redbourn	DP/83	1632-1917	1626-1649, 1685-1898	1617-1660, 1685-1906	1564-1869	1754-1810, 1823-1866	1617-1812, 1581-1793 BT	√	1753-1825
Reed	DP/84	1539-1766, 1813-1966	1539-1808, 1815-1988	1539-1766, 1813-1988	1800-1835	1755-1808, 1824-1988	1539-1738 C, 1539-1766 B	√	1746-1832
Rickmansworth	DP/85	1653-1920	1653-1966	1653-1925	1562-1854	1754-1806, 1864-1974	1569-1777 BT	√	1753-1825
[Rickmansworth: see also Chorleywood, Croxley Green, Mill End and West Hyde]									
Ridge	DP/86	1558-1927	1561-1836	1558-1932	1566-1869	1755-1813, 1825-1956	1567-1794 BT	√	1753-1825
Royston	DP/87	1662-1989	1662-1990	1772-1965	1802-1865	1754-1973	1662-1674	√	1746-1832
Rushden	DP/88	1607-1910	1607-1754, 1792-1992	1607-1992	1604-1869	1832, 1834	-	√	1746-1831
Rye Park (1937)	DP/24B	1907-1992	1911-1982	-	-	1911-1987	-	-	-
Sacombe	DP/89	1726-1903	1726-1979	1726-1937	1604-1884	1754-1811, 1824-1984	-	√	1715-1831, 1863-1891
St Albans									
Abbey	DP/90	1558-1708, 1743-1939	1558-1709, 1743-1940	1558-1708, 1743-1903	1570-1862	1743-1812	1558-1963	√	1753,1825
Christ Church (1859)	DP/91	1859-1964	1860-1983	-	1859-1869	-	-	-	-
St Luke (1986)	DP/93D	1940-1979	1971-1990	-	-	1973-1995	-	-	-
St Michael	DP/92	1643-1899	1643-1901	1643-1857	1572-1885	1754-1790	1572-1687 BT	√	1789-1825
St Paul (1910)	DP/93C	1905-1910	1910-1996	-	-	1910-1996	-	-	-
St Peter	DP/93	1558-1986	1558-1997	1558-1979	1571-1840	1754-1786, 1887-1995	1571-1766 BT, 1558-1812 B	-	1753-1825
St Saviour (1904)	DP/96A	1896-1924	1898-1944	-	-	1965-1979	-	-	-
St Stephen	DP/94	1596-1656, 1717-1975	1558-1646, 1697-1995	1558-1643, 1679-1962	1564-1869	1754-1983	1561-1633 C, 1561-1796 BT	-	1753-1825
[St Albans: see also Colney Heath, London Colney and Frogmore]									
[St Ippollitts: see Ippollitts]									
St Paul's Walden	DP/113	1559-1961	1559-1985	1558-1903	1561-1869	1754-1812, 1824-1969	1581-1800	√	1753-1827
Sandon	DP/95	1697-1960	1678-1993	1678-1992	1604-1858	1754-1874	-	√	1746-1832
Sandridge	DP/96	1559-1618, 1663-1967	1593-1977	1558-1913	1566-1871	1757-1812, 1824-1970	1558-1840, 1561-1800 BT	√	1753-1825

| Parish | Ref (HALS) | PARISH REGISTERS | | | | | | TAX | |
		Baptism	Marriage	Burial	BTs	Banns	Transc	Hearth	Land
Sarratt	DP/97	1560-1966	1562-1970	1562-1986	1566-1836	1755-1812, 1826-1983	1581-1796 BT	✓	1753-1825
Sawbridgeworth	DP/98	1558-1974	1558-1982	1558-1981	1800-1851	1754-1809, 1923-1990	-	✓	1712-1824
[Sawbridgeworth: see also High Wych]									
Shenley	DP/99	1653-1961	1653-1972	1653-1966	1604-1882	1936-1977	-	✓	1753-1830
Shephall	DP/100	1560-1977	1561-1992	1561-1812	1563-1869	1775-1795, 1823-1958	1581-1800 BT	✓	1753-1825
Standon	DP/101	1672-1985	1672-1985	1672-1946	1800-1813	1754-1809, 1836-1966	-	✓	1714-1831
[Standon: see also High Cross]									
Stanstead Abbots	DP/102	1695-1971	1754-2002	1679-1992	1800-1868	1754-1952	-	✓	1712-1831
Stanstead St Margarets	DP/103	1697-1717, 1759-1985	1703-1717, 1757-1995	1703-1717, 1762-1991	1813,1823, 1832	-	-	✓	1728-1831, 1863-1891
Stapleford	DP/104	1578-1979	1579-1985	1579-1980	1604-1888	1755-1810, 1824-1971	-	✓	1714-1831, 1863-1891
Stevenage									
St Nicholas	DP/105	1541-1961	1538-1599, 1660-1959	1543-1599, 1652-1983	1604-1868	1754-1823, 1833-1984	1653-1726	✓	1715-1831, 1864-1891
Holy Trinity	DP/105A	1956-1981	1960-1984	-	-	1982-1985	-	-	
St Hugh, Chells	DP/105B	1960-1984	1965-1980	-	-	1960-1983	-	-	
St Peter, Broadwater	DP/100A	1954-1979	1956-1988	-	-	1956-1992	-	-	
St Andrew, Bedwell	-	1951-1961	-	-	-	-	-	-	
All Saints, Pin Green	-	1967-1986	1974-1986	-	-	-	-	-	
Sunnyside (1909)	DP/74A	1886-1951	1909-1981	-	-	1901-1960	-	-	
Tewin	DP/106	1559-1926	1559-1728, 1755-1975	1559-1901	1604-1869	1755-1925	-	✓	1712-1831, 1863-1891
Therfield	DP/107	1538-1988	1538-1982	1538-1948	1604-1869	1754-1820, 1942-1952	-	✓	1746-1832
Thorley	DP/108	1539-1969	1539-1986	1539-1925	1800-1849	1754-1985	-	✓	1713-1831
Throcking	DP/109	1612-1812	1612-1836	1616-1809	1608-1869	1754-1977	1608-1836	✓	1746-1832
Thundridge	DP/110	1556-1913	1556-1994	1556-1885	1801-1842	1755-1778, 1829-1954	1556-1738	✓	1712-1831
[Tonwell: see Bengeo]									
Totteridge	DP/46B	1546, 1570-1903	1570-1841, 1898-1945	1570-1937	1604-1889	1754-1789, 1914-1969	1570-1837	✓	1715-1831, 1863-1891

Parish	Ref (HALS)	Baptism	Marriage	Burial	BTs	Banns	Transc	Hearth	Land
Tring	DP/111	1566-1959	1566-1941	1566-1969	1604-1869	1763-1812, 1855-1978	-	√	1746-1830
[Tring: see also Long Marston]									
Turnford St Clement	DP/29	1958-1998	1958-1997	-	-	1958-1978	-	-	-
Walkern	DP/114	1559-1930	1559-1985	1559-1963	1604-1869	1755-1838, 1897-1957	-	√	1715-1831, 1863-1891
Wallington	DP/115	1661-1991	1661-1975	1661-1991	1604-1869	1754-1914	1661-1753	√	1746-1812
Waltham Cross									
Holy Trinity & Christ Church (1855)	DP/29B	1855-1978	1855-1976	-	1856-1861	1886-1993	-	-	1711-1831
Ware									
St Mary	DP/116	1558-1984	1558-1717, 1730-1985	1558-1712, 1730-1966	1801-1843	1754-1828, 1857-1985	1558-1663 C, 1882-1893 C, 1834-1852 B	√	1712-1831
Christ Church (1858)	DP/116B	1858-1990	1858-1988	1915-1938	-	1858-1981	1841-1908	-	-
Wareside (1844)	DP/116A	1841-1920	1844-1959	1841-1908	1842	1844-1899	1841-1920	-	-
Waterford (1908)	DP/17B	1872-1979	1873-1996	1874-1979	-	1873-1980	-	-	-
Watford									
St Mary	DP/117	1539-1984	1539-1994	1539-1892	1570-1855	1809-1897, 1910-1987	1570-1800 BT	√	1753-1830
St Michael (1905)	DP/117C	1905-1982	1913-1991	1916-1917	-	1966-1984	-	-	-
St Andrew (1858)	DP/117A	1857-1962	1858-1967	-	-	1873-1974	-	-	-
Christ Church (1909)	DP/117D	1896-1961	1909-1975	-	-	1955-1987	-	-	-
St Mark	DP/117D	1931-1952	-	-	-	-	-	-	-
St George	DP/117D	1904-1931	-	-	-	-	-	-	-
St James (1913)	DP/117E	1909-1972	1913-1971	-	-	1913-1972	-	-	-
St John (1904)	DP/117K	-	-	1904-1962	-	-	-	-	-
St Peter	DP/117H	1936-1988	1944-1978	-	-	1944-1987	-	-	-
[Watford: see also Leavesden and Oxhey]									
Watton at Stone	DP/118	1560-1925	1560-1967	1560-1923	1604-1869	1754-1804, 1824-1989	-	√	1715-1831, 1863-1891
Welwyn	DP/119	1559-1978	1559-1741, 1754-1988	1558-1934	1604-1869	1754-1992	1559-1595 C, 1876-1919 C	√	1716-1831, 1863-1891
[Welwyn: see also Woolmer Green]									
Welwyn Garden City	DP/46C	1927-1952	1927-1980	-	-	1927-1967	-	-	-
West Hyde (1846)	DP/85B	1845-1961	1847-1982	1846-1926	-	1847-1896, 1948-1968	-	-	-

Parish	Ref (HALS)	PARISH REGISTERS						TAX	
		Baptism	Marriage	Burial	BTs	Banns	Transc	Hearth	Land
Westmill	DP/120	1580-1868	1562-1730, 1750-1838	1562-1930	1604-1869	1755-1947	1562-1837	✓	1716-1831
Weston	DP/121	1539-1932	1539-1937	1539-1897	1604-1869	1654-1707, 1754-1823	-	✓	1715-1831, 1863-1891
Wheathampstead	DP/122	1690-1962	1693-1973	1690-1950	1606-1869	1754-1781, 1949-1972	1604-1839	✓	1753-1829
[Wheathampstead: see also Harpenden]									
Widford	DP/123	1562-1978	1558-1996	1558-1894	1813-1868	1873-1984	-	✓	1714-1831
Wigginton	DP/124	1610-1683, 1705-1812	1610-1683, 1685-1748, 1818-1838	1610-1742, 1759-1812	1601-1869	-	-	✓	1746-1832
Wilbury (1980)	DP/75A	1942-1973	1968-1974	-	-	1968-1984	-	-	-
Willian	DP/125	1559-1990	1558-1989	1557-1934	1604-1872	1754-1812	-	✓	1715-1831, 1863-1891
Wilstone (1979)	DP/111B	-	-	-	-	1914-1929, 1963-1979	-	-	-
[Wilstone: see also Puttenham, Tring, Long Marston]									
[Woodhill: see Essendon]									
Woolmer Green	DP/119	1900-1959	1901-1981	-	-	-	-	-	-
Wormley	DP/126	1674-1974	1685-1985	1676-1963	1800-1869	1757-1831, 1912-1947	-	✓	1715-1831, 1863-1891
Wyddial	DP/127	1665-1995	1666-1963	1669-1995	1815-1849	1755-1807, 1849-1889	1665-1837	✓	1753-1832
Wymondley, Great	DP/128	1561-1691, 1710-1993	1561-1691, 1711-1901	1561-1690, 1710-1993	1604-1869	1755-1818	-	✓	1715-1831, 1863-1891
Wymondley, Little	DP/129	1577-1964	1750-1987	1628-1979	1629, 1719-1811	1823-1929	-	✓	1716-1831, 1863-1891

Appendix II
Nonconformist registers held at HALS

Apostolic
Ware; French Horn Lane: Bap 1832-40 (PC26/3)

Baptist
Berkhamsted, Gt: Bap 1799-1837, Bur 1801-83, 1905-14 (NB7/4/1-4)
Flaunden: Bap 1931-85, Mar 1931-85, Bur 1931-85
   (NB2/1 closed to inspection until 2010)
Hemel Hempstead: Bap 1785-1834, Bur 1785-1837 (PC26/1)
Hitchin; Tilehouse St: Bap 1717-1837, Bur 1785-1835 (PC26/2);
   Bap 1669-1840 (64351)
Markyate: Bap 1869-1947 (NB3/1)
Rickmansworth: Bap 1795-1836 (PC26/2)
St Albans; Dagnall Lane: Bap 1822-36, Bur 1822-37 (PC26/2)
Tring; Newmill: Bap 1793-1837 (index only)
Walden, King's; Coleman Green: Bap 1789-1837 (PC26/2)
Watford: Bap 1785-1837, Bur 1794-1837 (PC26/3)
Watford; Mount Zion Chapel: Mar 1964-86 (NB6/1)

Brethren
Barnet: Bap 1971-82 (NP1/1)
Croxley Green: Bap 1969-85 (NP2/1)

Congregational
Barkway: Bap 1812-37 (PC26/1); Bap 1858-1917, Mar 1899-1916,
   Bur 1797-1918, 1948-59 (PC434)
Barnet, New: Bap 1870-84, Mar 1871-80, 1914-17, Bur 1870-82 (NR15/1/1);
   Bap 1886-1917, Mar 1886-1914, Bur 1886-1917 (NR15/1/2-3);
   Bap 1933-63 (NR15/4/1-9)
Bishop's Stortford; Water Lane: Bap 1748-1836, Bur 1805-1855 (PC26/1);
   Bap 1837-59 (NR12/4/1); Bap 1860-1911, Mar 1861-1915 (NR12/1/1-2)
Boxmoor: Bap 1791-1837 (PC26/1); Bap 1885-1949, Mar 1919-47 (NC1/1/1);
   Bap 1948-65, Mar 1949-67 (NC1/4/1)
Cheshunt; Crossbrook Street: Bap 1729-99 (PC26/1); Bap 1848-1935, Mar 1864-1935
   (NC3/1/1); Bap 1914-55, Mar 1914-63 (NC3/4/1)
Hertford; Cowbridge: Bap 1785-1800, 1825-36 (PC26/2); Bap 1825-47 (NR14/1/2);
   Bap 1769-1809, Bur 1807-20 (NR14/4/1); Bap 1848-1934, Mar 1868-1921,
   Bur 1848-1940 (NR14/4/2)
Hitchin: Bap 1729-c1825 (64350) *see also Hitchin Independent*
Hoddesdon: Bap 1818-37 (PC26/2)

Knebworth; Park Lane: Bap 1947-54, Mar 1947-66, Bur 1947-67
    (NR16/4/1-2 access restricted); Bap 1887-1946, 1981-96, Mar 1897-1942,
    Bur 1890-1946 (NR16/1/2 access restricted)
Royston; Kneesworth Lane: Bap 1794-1828 (NR7/1/1); Bap 1839-1922,
    Mar 1839-1898, Bur 1842-93, 1904 (NR7/4/1)
Royston; John Street: Bap 1860-95 (NR7/4/3)
Ware; Church Street: Bap 1786-1836, Bur 1783-1834 (PC26/3); Bap 1778-1807,
    1868-73 (NR6/1/1)
Ware; High Street: Bap 1811-37 (PC26/3); Bap 1811-13, 1853-54 (NR6/1/2);
    Bap 1869-95, Mar 1880-97, Bur 1869-87 (NR6/1/3); Bap 1898-1942,
    Mar 1920-41, Bur 1920-42 (NR6/4/1)
Ware; Congregational Church: Bap 1942-61, Mar 1942-60, Bur 1942-60 (NR6/4/2)
Wheathampstead: Bap 1822-1906, Mar 1870-93, Bur 1822-1906 (NR10/1/1);
    Bap 1907-60, Mar 1913-70, Bur 1907-66 (NR10/1/2)

Evangelical
Bedmond; Christian Fellowship: Mar 1980 (NE1/1)
Borehamwood: Mar 1969-88 (NE2/1)
Redbourn: Mar 1988 (NE3/1)
St Albans: see below under Independent

Free Church
Letchworth: Bap 1928-66, Mar 1955 (NR5/1/1-12)

Countess of Huntingdon's Connexion
Cheshunt; College Chapel: Bap 1810-32, Bur 1832 (PC26/1)
Hertford; Back Street: Bap 1806-26 (PC26/2)

Independent
Ashwell; High Street: Bap 1797-1837, Bur 1798-1836 (PC26/1)
Barnet; Wood Street: Bap 1853-62, Mar 1853-60, Bur 1853-66 (NR1/3); Bap 1866-72,
    Mar 1868, Bur 1866-1871 (NR1/4); Bap 1874-1917, Bur 1974-1904 (NR1/5);
    Bap 1824-53 (NR1/6); Bur 1824-53 (NR1/7); Mar 1883-96 (NR1/9)
Berkhamsted, Gt: Bap 1787-1837, Bur 1793 (PC26/1)
Braughing: Bap 1812-36 (PC26/1)
Buntingford: Bap 1810-36, Bur 1824-35 (PC26/1)
Bushey: Bap 1816-37 (PC26/1); Bap 1817-1935, Mar 1839-1930,
    Bur 1838-1949 (NR2/2/2)
Cheshunt Street chapel: Bap 1782-1837 (PC26/1)
Hadham, Little: Bap 1804-36, Bur 1833-36 (PC26/2)
Harpenden: Bap 1819-21 (PC26/1); Bap 1834-36 (NR13/1/1A)
Hatfield; Park Street: Bap 1823-54, Bur 1846-1920 (transcript only)
Hitchin; Back Street: Bap 1772-1837, Bur 1786-1836 (PC26/2); Bap 1729-57
    (NR8/1/1); Bap 1847-84, Mar 1849-84, Bur 1849-64 (NR8/1/3);
    Bur 1837-46 (NR8/4/1)

Kings Langley; Zion Chapel: Bap 1834-37 (PC26/2)

Redbourn: Bap 1813-36 (PC26/2)

St Albans; Spicer Street (later Evangelical): Bap 1797-1837 (PC26/2);
　　Bap 1880-1914, Bur 1862-90 (NE4/1-2)

St Paul's Walden; Whitwell: Bap 1835, Bur 1834 (PC26/3)

Sandon; Redhill: Bap 1814-36 (PC26/2)

Sawbridgeworth: Bap 1817-36 (PC26/2)

Totteridge: Bap 1788-1837 (PC694); Bur 1800-85 (transcript only)

Walkern: Bap 1814-37 (PC26/2); Bur 1831-1962 (D/EX838)

Watford; Gilead Meeting: Bap 1808-30 (PC26/3)

Welwyn; Bethel Chapel: Bap 1793-1837 (PC26/3)

Methodist

(W = Wesleyan; P = Primitive)

Circuit registers

Biggleswade (Bedfordshire and Hertfordshire): see indexes at HALS

Bishop's Stortford & Hertford (W): Bap 1838-85 (NM10/9-10)

Hitchin (W): Bap 1838-1920 (NM4/52-54); Bap 1876-1901, 1905-17 (NM4/11)

Luton (Bedfordshire and Hertfordshire): see indexes at HALS

St Albans (W): Bap 1815-87 (NM5/41-43)

Saffron Walden (P) (Essex and Hertfordshire): Bap 1846-1908 (NM9/9-11)

Chapel registers

Abbots Langley, (W): Bap 1947-61 (NM7C/45-46)

Ashwell (W): Bap 1873-1970, Mar 1942-71 (NM11C/1-2)

Barnet, New; Station Road (W): Mar 1918-62 (NM1B/5-10)

Berkhamsted; Cowper Road (W): Bap 1910-55, Mar 1900-52 (NM3C/1-2)

Bishop's Stortford (W): Bap 1827-37 (PC26/1)

Borehamwood (W): Mar 1959-75 (NM1F/6-7)

Chorleywood (P): Bap 1948-63, Mar 1957 (NM7L/1-2)

Croxley Green (P): Bap 1948-62 (NM7M/14)

Flamstead (W): Bap 1861-1959 (NM2G/1)

Harpenden; High Street (W): Bap 1875-1960, Mar 1890-1940 (NM2B/1/1-5)

Harpenden; Kinsbourne Green (W): Mar 1937-39 (NM2A/1)

Harpenden; Highfield: Mar 1934-85 (NM2M/1-4)

Hemel Hempstead (W): Bap 1836-37 (PC26/1)

Hertford (W): Bap 1885-1971 (NM10A/8)

Hinxworth (W): Bap 1870-1960 (NM11B/2)

Hitchin; Brand Street (W): Bap 1835-37 (PC26/2); Mar 1870-91 (NM4A/38)

Hitchin; Walworth: Bap 1958-77 (NM4L/3)

Ickleford (W): Bap 1938-77 (NM4G/5)

Offley (W): Bap 1957-70, Mar 1945-71 (NM4H/2-3)

St Albans (W): Bap 1825-37 (PC26/2)

Sewardstone (Essex) (W): Bap 1932-68 (NM10E/8)

Stevenage; Chells: Mar 1969-75 (NM6B/1)
Two Waters (W): Bap 1910-60 (transcript only)
Waltham Abbey (Essex) (W): Bap 1860-1967, Mar 1911-46 (NM10F/8-10)
Watford; Carpenders Park: Bap 1976-79 (NM7R/1)
Watford; Queen's Road (W): Mar 1903-66 (NM7A/1-8)
Watford; Queen's Road (P): Mar 1939-41 (NM7J/3)
Watford; St Albans Road (P): Mar 1927-70 (NM7I/1-4)

Presbyterian
St Albans; Dagnall Lane: Bap 1751-1836 (PC26/2)
Ware; Swan Yard: Bap 1787-1807 (PC26/2)

Quaker
Quarterly meeting registers
Herts. and Beds.: Bap 1643-1838 (NQ1/5B/1); Bap 1656-1796, Mar 1656-1796,
   Bur 1656-1796 (NQ1/5B/2); Mar 1658-1836 (NQ1/5C/1);
   Bur 1656-1838 (NQ1/5D/1)
Monthly meeting registers
Cottered: Bap 1656-1775, Mar 1663-1721, Bur 1659-1778 (PC26/5)
Hertford: Bap 1718-1835, Mar 1713, 1760-1836, Bur 1729-1837 (PC26/5)
Hitchin: Bap 1643-1775, Mar 1658-1771, Bur 1660-1775 (PC26/6)
St Albans: Bap 1661-1837, Mar 1690-1834, Bur 1677-1837 (PC26/5)

Appendix III
Cemeteries and crematoria within Hertfordshire
with contact details

Broxbourne Borough Council
Cheshunt Cemetery (records from 1856, no public access): Bury Green Road, Cheshunt.
Hoddesdon Cemetery (records from 1883, no public access): Ware Road, Hoddesdon.
Contact (in writing only): The Cemetery Office, Broxbourne Borough Council,
Bishops College, Churchgate, Cheshunt, EN8 9XF.

Dacorum Borough Council
Heath Lane Cemetery (records from 1878, limited public access during office hours):
   Heath Lane, Hemel Hempstead.
Kingshill Cemetery (records from 1947, limited public access during office hours):
   Kingshill Way, Berkhamsted.
Tring Cemetery (records from 1894, limited public access during office hours):
   Aylesbury Road, Tring.
Woodwells Cemetery (records from 1960, limited public access during office hours):
   Buncefield Lane, Hemel Hempstead.
Contact: The Cemeteries Manager, Dacorum Borough Council, Woodwells Cemetery,
Buncefield Lane, Hemel Hempstead, HP2 7HY (tel: 01442 252856).

East Herts District
Bishop's Stortford Cemetery (Old Cemetery, records from 1855; New Cemetery, records
   from 1946): Cemetery Road, Bishop's Stortford.
   Contact: The Town Clerk, Town Council Office, The Old Monastery, Windhill,
   Bishop's Stortford, CM23 2ND (tel: 01279 652274).
Hertford Cemetery (records from 1909, public access during normal working hours):
   North Road, Hertford (NB: earlier burials in this cemetery are recorded in St Andrew's
   church burial registers held at HALS Ref. DP/49).
   Contact: The Town Clerk, Hertford Town Council, The Castle, Hertford, SG14 1HR
   (tel: 01992 552885).
   The Town Clerk also has responsibility for the maintenance of four closed
   churchyards in the town.
Sawbridgeworth Cemetery (1951): Cambridge Road, Sawbridgeworth.
   Contact: The Town Clerk, Sawbridgeworth Town Council, Sayebury Manor,
   Bell Street, Sawbridgeworth (tel: 01279 724537).
Ware Cemetery (records from 1857, public access during office hours by appointment):
   Watton Road, Ware (entrance off Wulfrath Way).
   Contact: Ware Town Council offices, The Priory, Ware SG12 9AL (tel: 01920 460316).

Hertsmere Borough Council

Elstree Cemetery (records from 1962, public access at council offices by appointment):
Allum Lane, Elstree. Allum Lane is a lawn cemetery.
Contact: The Leisure Administration Officer, Client and Customer Services,
Hertsmere Borough Council, Civic Offices, Elstree Way, Borehamwood WD6 1WA
(tel: 020 8207 7497).

North Hertfordshire District Council

Baldock Cemetery (records from c.1900, public access by appointment):
The Sycamores, Baldock.
Hitchin Cemetery (records from c.1855, public access by appointment):
St John's Road, Hitchin.
Knebworth Cemetery (records from c.1985, public access by appointment):
Wadnall Way, Knebworth.
Letchworth Cemetery (records from c.1920, public access by appointment):
Icknield Way, Letchworth.
Royston Cemetery (records from c.1900, public access by appointment):
Melbourn Road, Royston.
Contact: The Legal and Administration Services Department, North Hertfordshire
District Council, Gernon Road, Letchworth SG6 3JF (tel: 01462 474000).
The records are computerised so personal searches are unnecessary.
Written or telephone enquiries preferred.

City and District of St Albans

Hatfield Road Cemetery (records from 1884, public access by appointment):
Hatfield Road, St Albans.
London Road Cemetery (records from 1980, public access by appointment):
London Road, St Albans.
Westfield Road Cemetery (records from 1926, public access by appointment):
Westfield Road, Harpenden.
Contact: The Cemetery Superintendent, St Albans District Council,
Cemetery Office, 178 Hatfield Road, St Albans AL1 4LU (tel: 01727 819362).
Office hours: Monday to Thursday 8 am - 4.30 pm; Friday 8 am - 3.30 pm;
office closed at weekends but cemetery gates open at 8 am
(10 am on Sundays and Bank Holidays) and close from 4.30 pm (later in the summer).
The registers from all the cemeteries are kept at Hatfield Road.

Stevenage Borough Council

Almond Road Cemetery (records from 1944, no public access): Almond Road, Stevenage.
Weston Road Cemetery (records from 1988, no public access): Weston Road, Stevenage.
Contact: The Cemeteries and Amenities Officer, Stevenage Borough Council,
Weston Road Cemetery, Stevenage SG1 3RP (tel: 01438 367109).
Records can be consulted for researchers, and they can view the records
under supervision.

Three Rivers District Council

Rickmansworth Road Cemetery: Rickmansworth Road, Rickmansworth.
Woodcock Hill Cemetery: Woodcock Hill, Rickmansworth.
Contact: The Environmental Protection Section,
Three Rivers District Council, Three Rivers House, Northway,
Rickmansworth WD3 1RL (tel: 01923 776611).
The burial registers 1857-1961 have been deposited at HALS (HALS: Off Acc 546).

Watford Borough Council

North Watford Cemetery (records from 1932, no public access):
  North Western Avenue, Watford.
Vicarage Road Cemetery (records from 1858, no public access): Vicarage Road, Watford.
Contact: The Cemetery Office, North Watford Cemetery, North Western Avenue,
Watford WD2 6AW (tel: 01923 672157). Information can be supplied by telephone.

Welwyn Hatfield District Council

Hatfield Hyde Cemetery (records from 1923, supervised public access):
  Hollybush Lane, Welwyn Garden City.
The Lawn Cemetery (records from 1984, supervised public access): Southway, Hatfield.
Contact: The Director of Environmental Services, Welwyn Hatfield District Council,
Council Offices, The Campus, Welwyn Garden City AL8 6AE (tel: 01707 331212).

Crematoria

Harwood Park Crematorium and Cemetery (records from 1997).
  Contact: The Manager and Registrar, Harwood Park Crematorium, Watton Road,
  Stevenage SG2 8XT (tel: 01438 815555).
West Herts Crematorium (1959).
  Contact: The Manager and Registrar, West Herts Crematorium Joint Committee, High
  Elms Lane, Garston WD21 7JS (tel: 01923 673285).

Private (Jewish) cemeteries

Adath Yisroel Jewish Cemetery, Silver Street, Cheshunt (1966).
  Contact: Adath Yisroel Burial Society, 40 Queen Elizabeth's Walk,
  Stamford Hill, London N16 0HJ.
Western (Jewish) Cemetery, Bullscross Ride, Cheshunt (1968).
  Contact: Joint Jewish Burial Society, Alyth Gardens, Finchley Road, London NW11.
Bushey Jewish Cemetery, Little Bushey Lane, Bushey (1947).
  Contact: United Synagogue Burial Society, 735 High Road, London N12 0US.

Appendix IV
Where to look for Wills:
Archdeaconry Courts in Hertfordshire to 1858

Please refer to the map of Hertfordshire showing ecclesiastical boundaries, pages 8-9,
and to Chapter 9, Printed Sources, for a listing of will abstracts in Brigg, W., Hertfordshire
Genealogist and Antiquary.

Archdeaconry of Middlesex (Essex and Herts Division)
Location of records: Essex Record Office, Wharf Road, Chelmsford, Essex CM2 6YT
Jurisdiction: 25 Hertfordshire parishes to the east of the A10
Holdings: Wills, 1602-1857; will registers, 1538-1858; admons, 1669-1857
Name indexes have been published and are available at HALS.

Archdeaconry of St Albans
Location of records: HALS
Jurisdiction: 22 Hertfordshire parishes mostly in the vicinity of St Albans
                          and the Buckinghamshire parishes of Aston Abbots, Grandborough,
                          Little Horwood and Winslow
Holdings: Original wills, 1518-1858; will registers, 1415-1857;
                          inventories, 1518-1764; only one probate account dated 1484 is
                          known to survive copied into a will register (HALS: 2AR 43v-44v);
                          admons, 1540-1857 (HALS: ASA 26)
An index to testators is available.

Archdeaconry of Huntingdon (Hitchin Division)
Location of records: HALS and Huntingdon Record Office, Grammar School Walk,
                          Huntingdon PE18 6LF
Jurisdiction: 76 Hertfordshire parishes
Holdings: HALS: original wills, 1585-1857; will registers, 1557-1843;
                          inventories, 1568-1789 (HALS: AHH 22 includes some admons);
                          admons and accounts, 1609-1857 (HALS: AHH 23).
                          Huntingdon: will registers, 1479-1652 containing
                          Hertfordshire entries
There is an index of testators for HALS' holdings. A microfilm of the Huntingdon registers dated
1566-1609 is held at HALS. A manuscript index 1479-1652 of Hertfordshire testators whose
wills are held at Huntingdon is also available.

Peculiar Court of the Dean and Chapter of St Paul's Cathedral
Location of records: Guildhall Library, Aldermanbury, London EC2P 2EJ
Jurisdiction: Albury, Brent Pelham and Furneux Pelham
Holdings: Wills, 1660-1837; will registers, 1535-1837; probate and
                          administration act books, 1646-1837; inventories, 1660-1725;
                          accounts of fees, 1748-80
An index of Hertfordshire testators 1560-1837 is held at HALS.

Commissary Court of London for Essex and Herts

Location of records: Essex Record Office, Wharf Road, Chelmsford CM2 6YT

Jurisdiction: Bishop's Stortford, Little Hadham, Much Hadham,
Little Hormead and Royston

Holdings: Wills, 1441-1858; will registers, 1553-1858; admons, 1669-1858

Name indexes to testators have been published and are held at HALS.

Consistory Court of the Bishop of Lincoln

Location of records: Lincolnshire Archives, St Rumbold Street,
Lincoln LN2 5AB

Jurisdiction: Whole of Hertfordshire except the Archdeaconry of
Middlesex before 1550 (St Albans Archdeaconry had an
exempt jurisdiction from 1163); after 1550 the area of the
Archdeaconry of Huntingdon only, to 1845

Holdings: The following all contain Hertfordshire wills: bishops'
registers, 1320-1547; other diocesan manuscripts, 1489-1588;
will registers (and some original wills), 1506-1858;
inventories, 1508-1851; administrations, c.1569-1858;
administration accounts, 1559-1853

*A published index to testators is held at HALS. A number of other published
and unpublished indexes to Lincoln wills are also available.*

Consistory Court of the Bishop of London

Location of records: London Metropolitan Archives, 40 Northampton Road,
Clerkenwell, London EC1R 0HB

Jurisdiction: The whole diocese of London (including the Archdeaconry of
St Albans from 1550) except the peculiars (these were parishes
or churches with particular jurisdiction and the power to grant
administration or probate of wills exempt from the usual ecclesiastical
authority). This court would replace the lower courts when they were
temporarily suspended, for example, during the bishop's visitation;
this happened in the St Albans archdeaconry for three months
every four years.

Holdings: Original wills and administrations, 1507-1858; registers of wills
and administrations, 1492, 1514-1858; vicar-generals' books
which include probate and administration acts, 1521-1685;
very few probate inventories have survived for this court.

*An index of Hertfordshire testators 1514-1811 is held at HALS
(this is worth checking if a St Albans will cannot be found amongst the archdeaconry records).*

Prerogative Court of Canterbury (PCC)

Location of records: Public Record Office, Ruskin Avenue, Kew, Richmond,
Surrey TW9 4DU (microfilm copies of all PCC
wills are held at the FRC)

Jurisdiction: The Province of Canterbury

Holdings: Original wills, 1383-1858 (PRO: PROB 10); will registers,
1383-1858 (PRO: PROB 11); administration act books, 1559-1858
(PRO: PROB 6); inventories, 1417-1782 (but few before 1660);
some accounts, 1667-1722 (PRO: PROB 5)

*Name indexes have been published covering wills 1383-1700, 1750-1800 and on
fiche for 1701-49 and 1853-57, and admons 1559-1700 and 1750-1800, all available
at HALS. The PRO has begun to place PROB 11 records on the internet:* <www.pro.gov.uk>.

Appendix V
Hertfordshire library holdings

The libraries listed below hold copies on microfilm of parish registers and census returns for their area, and on microfiche of the IGI. It is advisable to telephone the library concerned to check on the availability of a microfilm/fiche reading machine before making your visit, or if it is particularly important that a book or other material is available when you call. Telephone: 01438 737333 (01923 471333 from area codes 01923 or 020). The library holdings of local newspapers can be found online at <www.hertsdirect.org/hals>; stock of local trade directories can be found in the online library catalogue at <www.hertsdirect.org/libraries>.

Baldock Library, Simpson Drive, Baldock, Herts SG7 6DH
Parish registers
Ashwell; Baldock; Hinxworth; Newnham
Census
Aston 1841; *Ayot Green* 1841; *Ayot St Lawrence* 1841; *Baldock* 1841-1901; *Benington* 1841; *Bygrave* 1851, 1871; *Caldecote* 1851, 1871; *Clothall* 1851, 1871; *Datchworth* 1841; *Digswell* 1841; *Graveley* 1841-51, 1871; *Gt Wymondley* 1851; *Hatfield* 1841; *Knebworth* 1841-51, 1871; *Letchworth* 1851; *Lt Wymondley* 1851; *Newnham* 1851, 1871; *Norton* 1851, 1871; *Radwell* 1851, 1871; *Stevenage* 1851; *Weston* 1851; *Willian* 1851

Bishop's Stortford Library, 6 The Causeway, Bishop's Stortford, Herts CM23 2EJ
Parish registers
Albury; Bishop's Stortford; Braughing; Eastwick; Furneux Pelham; Gilston; Lt Hadham; Sawbridgeworth; Standon; Stocking Pelham; Thorley
Census
1881 census (fiche) whole of Hertfordshire; Essex
Albury 1841-1901; *Anstey* 1841-61,1891-1901; *Ardeley* 1901; *Aspenden* 1841,1861, 1891-1901; *Barkway* 1841; *Barley* 1841; *Berden* (Essex) 1861-71,1891-1901; *Birchanger* (Essex) 1861-71,1891-1901; *Bishop's Stortford* 1841-1901; *Braughing* 1841-1901; *Brent Pelham* 1841-1901; *Broadfield* 1901; *Broxbourne* 1851; *Buckland* 1841,1901 (part); *Buntingford* 1901; *Colliers End* 1901; *Cottered* 1901; *Eastwick* 1841-51; *Elsenham* (Essex) 1861-71,1891-1901; *Farnham* (Essex) 1861-71,1891-1901; *Furneux Pelham* 1841-1901; *Gilston* 1841-51; *Gt Amwell* 1851; *Gt Hallingbury* (Essex) 1861,1891-1901; *Gt Hormead* 1841-61,1891-1901; *Gt Munden* 1851-1901; *Henham* (Essex) 1861-71,1891-1901; *High Cross* 1901; *High Wych* 1901; *Hockerill* 1841-1901; *Hoddesdon* 1851; *Hunsdon* 1841-51; *Layston* 1841,1861,1891-1901; *Lt Hadham* 1841-1901; *Lt Hallingbury* 1861-71,1901; *Lt Hormead* 1841-61,1891-1901; *Lt Munden* 1851-1901 (part); *Manuden* (Essex) 1851-71,1891-1901; *Meesden* 1841,1891-1901; *Mentley* 1901; *Much Hadham* 1841-1901; *Nuthampstead* 1841; *Old Hall Green* 1901; *Puckeridge* 1901; *Rushden* 1901; *St Edmund's College* 1901; *Sandon* 1901;

Sawbridgeworth 1841,1861-71,1891; *Standon* 1841-1901; *Stanstead Abbotts* 1841;
Stanstead St Margarets 1851; *Stansted Mountfitchet* (Essex) 1861-71,1891-1901;
Stocking Pelham 1841-1901; *Thorley* 1841,1861-71,1891-1901;
Throcking 1841,1861,1891-1901; *Thundridge* 1841-61; *Ugley* (Essex) 1861-71,1891-1901;
Wallington 1901; *Ware* 1841-61; *Westmill* 1841,1861,1891-1901; *Whempstead* 1901;
Widford 1841-51; *Wormley* 1851; *Wyddial* 1841,1861,1891-1901
IGI
Hertfordshire (fiche, 1984 edition)

Bovingdon Library, High Street, Bovingdon, Herts HP3 0HJ
Census
Bovingdon 1871, 1891 (photocopies)

Bushey Library, Sparrows Herne, Bushey, Herts WD23 1FA
IGI
Hertfordshire (fiche, 1984 edition)

Hatfield Library, Queensway, Hatfield, Herts AL10 0LT
Parish registers
Bayford; Essendon; North Mymms

Hemel Hempstead Library, Combe Street, Hemel Hempstead, Herts HP1 1HJ
Parish registers
*Abbots Langley; Aldbury; Berkhamsted; Bovingdon; Flamstead; Gt Gaddesden; Hemel
Hempstead; Kings Langley; Langleybury; Long Marston; Northchurch; Puttenham; Sunnyside;
Tring; Wigginton*
Census
1881 census (fiche) whole of Hertfordshire; Buckinghamshire
Abbots Langley 1891-1901; *Aldbury* 1841-1901; *Amersham* (Bucks, part) 1841;
Apsley End 1891-1901; *Beaconsfield* (Bucks, part) 1841; *Bedmond* 1891-1901;
Berkhamstead 1841-1901; *Bourne End* 1841-61,1891-1901; *Bovingdon* 1841-1901;
Boxmoor 1841-1901; *Bushey* (part) 1841; *Caddington* (part) 1841; *Chesham* (Bucks) 1901;
Chipperfield 1841-1901(part); *Coleshill* 1841; *Cow Roast* 1841,1891-1901;
Flamstead 1841-1901; *Flaunden* 1841-1901; *Frithsden* 1841-61,1891-1901;
Gt Gaddesden 1841-1901; *Gt Missenden* (Bucks) 1901; *Gubblecote* 1851,1901;
Harpenden (part) 1841; *Hemel Hempstead* 1841-1901; *Hunton Bridge* 1891,1901;
Kings Langley 1841-1901; *Langleybury* 1891; *Leverstock Green* 1841-61,1891-1901 (part);
Lt Gaddesden 1841-1901; *Lt Heath* 1891; *Long Marston* 1851-61,1891-1901;
Markyate 1841-1901; *Marsworth* 1851-61,1891-1901; *Nash Mills* 1841-61,1891-1901;
Nettleden 1841-61,1891-1901; *Northchurch* 1841-1901; *Piccotts End* 1841-51,1901;
Pimlico 1891; *Pitstone* 1851-61,1891-1901; *Potten End* 1841-1901;
Puttenham 1841-61,1891-1901; *Shenley* 1841; *Studham* (Beds) 1841; *Tring* 1841-1901;
Two Waters 1841-1901; *Wheathampstead* 1841 (part); *Wigginton* 1841-61,1891-1901;
Wilstone 1851-61,1891-1901
IGI
English Counties (fiche, 1992 edition)

Hitchin Library, Paynes Park, Hitchin, Herts SG5 1EW
Parish registers
Ayot St Lawrence; Ayot St Peter; Codicote; Gt Wymondley; Hexton; Hitchin; Ickleford; Kimpton; King's Walden; Lilley; Offley; Pirton; St Ippollitts; St Paul's Walden
Census
Ardeley 1881; *Ashwell* 1881; *Aston* 1891; *Baldock* 1881; *Barkway* 1881; *Barley* 1881;
Bayford 1891; *Bendish* 1881; *Bengeo* 1891; *Benington* 1891; *Bramfield* 1891;
Broadfield 1881; *Buntingford* 1881; *Bygrave* 1881; *Clothall* 1881; *Codicote* 1881-91;
Datchworth 1891; *Gosmore* 1891-1901; *Graveley* 1881; *Gt Chishall* (Cambs) 1881;
Gt Wymondley 1881-91; *Guilden Morden* (Cambs) 1881; *Hertford* 1891; *Hexton* 1881-1901;
Heydon (Cambs) 1881; *Hinxworth* 1881; *Hitchin* 1841-1901; *Holwell* 1881-1901;
Ickleford 1881-1901; *Kelshall* 1881; *Kimpton* 1881-1901; *King's Walden* 1881-1901;
Knebworth 1881; *Langley* 1881-1901; *Lilley* 1881-1901; *Lt Almshoe* 1891; *Lt Chishall* 1881;
Lt Wymondley 1881-91; *Newsells* 1881; *Newnham* 1881; *Norton* 1881; *Offley* 1881-1901;
Pirton 1881-1901; *Preston* 1891-1901; *Radwell* 1881; *Reed* 1881; *Royston* 1881;
Rushden 1881; *St Ippollitts* 1881-1901; *St Paul's Walden* 1891-1901; *Sandon* 1881;
Shephall 1881; *Shillington* (Beds) 1901 (part); *Stapleford* 1891;
Steeple Morden (Cambs) 1881; *Stevenage* 1881-91; *Tewin* 1891; *Therfield* 1881;
Walkern 1891; *Wallington* 1881; *Walsworth* 1901; *Watton* 1891; *Westmill* 1881;
Weston 1881-91; *Whitwell* 1891-1901; *Willian* 1881; *Wyddial* 1881
IGI
Hertfordshire (fiche - 1988 edition)

Hoddesdon Library, 98a High Street, Hoddesdon, Herts EN11 8HD
Parish registers
Broxbourne; Cheshunt; Gt Amwell; Hoddesdon; Lt Amwell
Census
Albury 1891; *Amwell End* 1891-1901; *Appleby Street* (Cheshunt) 1881, 1901; *Ardeley* 1891;
Aspenden 1891; *Bakers End* 1891; *Barwick* 1891-1901 (part); *Bayford* 1841;
Bengeo 1841, 1891; *Bentfield End* 1891; *Birch Green* 1891-1901; *Birchanger* (Essex) 1891;
Bishop's Stortford 1891; *Braughing* 1891; *Brickendon* 1841, 1891; *Bromley* 1891;
Broxbourne 1841, 1891-1901; *Buckland* 1891; *Chapmore End* 1891; *Cheshunt* 1841-1901;
Cold Christmas 1891-1901; *Colliers End* 1891; *Cottered* 1891; *Dane End* 1891;
Easneye 1891-1901; *Eastwick* 1891-1901; *Elsenham* (Essex) 1891; *Enfield* 1901;
Essendon 1841; *Farnham* (Essex) 1891; *Flamstead End* 1891-1901; *Furneux Pelham* 1891;
Gilston 1891-1901; *Gt Amwell* 1841, 1891-1901; *Gt Hallingbury* (Essex) 1891;
Gt Hormead 1891; *Gt Munden* 1891; *Green End* 1891; *Haileybury* 1891-1901;
Hammond Street 1881, 1901; *Hatfield* 1891; *Haultwick* 1891; *Henham* (Essex) 1891;
Hertford 1891; *Hertford Heath* 1891-1901; *Hertingfordbury* 1841, 1891; *High Cross* 1891;
Hockerill 1891; *Hoddesdon* 1841, 1891-1901; *Hunsdon* 1891-1901; *Layston* 1891;
Lemsford 1891; *Lt Amwell* 1841, 1891; *Lt Berkhamstead* 1841, 1891; *Lt Hadham* 1891;
Lt Hallingbury (Essex) 1891; *Lt Hormead* 1891; *Lt Munden* 1891; *Manuden* (Essex) 1891;
Mentley 1891; *Much Hadham* 1891; *Newgate Street* 1891; *Old Hall Green* 1891;
Puckeridge 1891; *Rushden* 1891; *Sandon* 1891; *Sawbridgeworth* 1891; *Standon* 1891;
Stanstead Abbotts 1891-1901; *Stanstead St Margarets* 1841, 1891-1901;
Stansted Mountfitchet (Essex) 1891; *Stapleford* 1841; *Stocking Pelham* 1891; *Tewin* 1841;

Theobalds 1891-1901; *Thorley* 1891; *Throcking* 1891; *Thundridge* 1891-1901;
Tonwell 1891; *Turnford* 1881-1901; *Ugley* (Essex) 1891; *Wadesmill* 1891-1901;
Wallington 1891; *Waltham Abbey* (Essex) 1851; *Waltham Cross* 1851, 1871, 1891-1901;
Ware 1891-1901; *Waterford* 1891; *Well Pond Green* 1891; *Westmill* 1891;
Whempstead 1891; *Widford* 1891-1901; *Wormley* 1841, 1891-1901; *Wyddial* 1891

Kings Langley Library, The Nap, Kings Langley, Herts WD4 8ET
Census (copies belonging to Kings Langley Local History Society but available for public
consultation; please telephone the library to make an appointment to view)
Chipperfield 1841-51, 1871; Kings Langley 1841-51, 1871

Letchworth Library, Broadway, Letchworth, Herts SG6 3PF
Parish registers
Letchworth; Radwell; Willian
Census
Abbots Langley 1841; *Aldenham* 1841; *Baldock* 1851-91; *Barnet* 1841; *Bramfield* 1841;
Bygrave 1851-61, 1881-91; *Caldecote* 1851-61, 1881-91; *Chipping Barnet* 1841;
Clothall 1851-61, 1881-91; *Codicote* 1841; *East Barnet* 1841; *Elstree* 1841;
Graveley 1851-61, 1881-91; *Gt Munden* 1841; *Gt Wymondley* 1841-51; *Hexton* 1841;
Knebworth 1851-91; *Letchworth* 1841-1901; *Lt Munden* 1841; *Lt Wymondley* 1841-51;
Newnham 1841-61, 1881-91; *Northaw* 1841; *Norton* 1841-91; *Radwell* 1851-61, 1881-91;
Redbourn 1841; *Rickmansworth* 1841; *Ridge* 1841; *Sacombe* 1841; *St Paul's Walden* 1841;
Shephall 1851, 1871, 1891; *Stevenage* 1841-51, 1871; *Totteridge* 1841; *Walkern* 1841;
Watton 1841; *Welwyn* 1841; *Weston* 1841-51; *Whitwell* 1841; *Willian* 1841-91

Oakmere Library, High Street, Potters Bar, Herts EN6 5BZ
Census
Arkley 1901; *Barnet* 1901; *Chipping Barnet* 1901; *Colney Heath* 1901 (part);
East Barnet 1901; *Elstree* 1901; *Finchley* (Middx) 1901; *Friern Barnet* (Middx) 1901;
Lyonsdown 1901; *Monken Hadley* 1901; *Potters Bar* 1901; *Ridge* 1901; *Shenley* 1901;
South Mimms 1901; *Totteridge* 1901

Rickmansworth Library, High Street, Rickmansworth, Herts WD3 1EH
IGI
Hertfordshire (fiche, 1988 edition)

Royston Library, Market Hill, Royston, Herts SG8 9JN
Parish registers
*Ashwell; Aspenden; Barkway; Barley; Buckland; Kelshall; Reed; Royston; Therfield; Throcking;
Wyddial*
Census
Abingdon Piggotts (Cambs) 1891-1901; *Ashwell* 1891-1901; *Baldock* 1891;
Barkway 1891-1901; *Barley* 1891-1901; *Barrington* (Cambs) 1891-1901;
Bassingbourn (Cambs) 1891-1901; *Buckland* 1891-1901; *Bygrave* 1891; *Caldecote* 1891;
Clothall 1891; *Fowlmere* (Cambs) 1891-1901; *Foxton* (Cambs) 1891-1901; *Graveley* 1891;
Gt Chishall (Cambs) 1901; *Guilden Morden* (Cambs) 1891-1901;

Heydon (Cambs) 1891-1901; *Hinxworth* 1891-1901; *Kelshall* 1891-1901; *Knebworth* 1891;
Kneesworth (Cambs) 1891-1901; *Letchworth* 1891; *Litlington* (Cambs) 1891-1901;
Lt Chishall 1891-1901; *Melbourn* (Cambs) 1891-1901; *Meldreth* (Cambs) 1891-1901;
Newnham 1891; *Norton* 1891; *Nuthampstead* 1901; *Radwell* 1891; *Reed* 1891-1901;
Royston 1891-1901; *Shephall* 1891; *Shepreth* (Cambs) 1891-1901;
Shingay (Cambs) 1891-1901; *Steeple Morden* (Cambs) 1891-1901; *Stevenage* 1891;
Therfield 1891-1901; *Thriplow* (Cambs) 1891-1901; *Wendy* (Cambs) 1901;
Whaddon (Cambs) 1891; *Willian* 1891

St Albans Central Library, The Maltings, St Albans, Herts AL1 3JQ
Parish registers
Colney Heath; Harpenden; London Colney; Redbourn; St Albans; Sandon; Sandridge;
Wheathampstead
Census
1881 census (fiche) whole of Hertfordshire
Bricket Wood 1901 (part); *Chiswell Green* 1901; *Colney Heath* 1901 (part); *Frogmore* 1901;
Harpenden 1851,1881,1901; *Hertford* 1841; *Leverstock Green* 1901 (part);
London Colney 1901; *Pimlico* 1901; *Redbourn* 1851,1881,1901; *St Albans* 1841-81,1901;
St Peter's 1841-1901; *St Michael's* 1841 (incomplete),1851,1871-1901;
St Stephen's 1851-81,1901; *Sandridge* 1851,1881,1901; *Tyttenhanger* 1901;
Wheathampstead 1851,1881,1901

Stevenage Central Library, Southgate, Stevenage, Herts SG1 1HD
Parish registers
Aston; Benington; Datchworth; Graveley; Shephall; Walkern; Weston
Census
1881 census (fiche) whole of Hertfordshire
Abbots Langley 1841; *Albury* 1841-51; *Aldenham* 1841; *Anstey* 1841-51, 1891;
Ardeley 1841-51, 1891; *Ashwell* 1841-51; *Aspenden* 1841-51, 1891; *Aston* 1841-1901;
Ayot St Lawrence 1841-51; *Ayot St Peter* 1841-51; *Baldock* 1841-61, 1881-1901;
Barkway 1841-51; *Barley* 1841-51; *Barnet* 1841; *Bassingbourn* (Cambs) 1841;
Bayford 1851, 1901; *Bengeo* 1851, 1901; *Benington* 1841-1901; *Berden* (Essex) 1851;
Birchanger (Essex) 1851; *Bishop's Stortford* 1841-51; *Bramfield* 1841-51, 1901;
Braughing 1841-51; *Brent Pelham* 1841-51; *Brickendon* 1841-51, 1901; *Broadfield* 1891;
Broxbourne 1841-51; *Buckland* 1841-51, 1891; *Bygrave* 1841-61, 1881-1901;
Caldecote 1841-61, 1881-1901; *Chapmore End* 1901; *Cheshunt* 1841;
Chipping Barnet 1841; *Clothall* 1841-61, 1881-1901; *Codicote* 1841-51, 1901;
Cottered 1841-51, 1891; *Datchworth* 1841-1901; *Digswell* 1841-51; *East Barnet* 1841;
Eastwick 1841-51; *Elstree* 1841; *Essendon* 1841-51; *Farnham* (Essex) 1851;
Furneux Pelham 1841-51; *Gilston* 1851; *Graveley* 1841-61, 1881-1901; *Gt Amwell* 1841-51;
Gt Chishall (Cambs) 1851; *Gt Hallingbury* (Essex) 1851; *Gt Hormead* 1841, 1891;
Gt Munden 1841-51; *Gt Wymondley* 1841-1901; *Guilden Morden* (Cambs) 1841-51;
Hatfield 1841-51; *Henham* (Essex) 1851; *Hertford* 1841-51, 1901;
Hertingfordbury 1841-51, 1901; *Hexton* 1841; *Heydon* (Cambs) 1851; *Hinxworth* 1841-51;
Hitchin 1841-61; *Hoddesdon* 1841-51; *Holwell* 1861; *Hunsdon* 1851; *Ickleford* 1841, 1861;
Kelshall 1841-51; *Kimpton* 1841-61; *King's Walden* 1841-61; *Knebworth* 1841-1901;

Kneesworth (Cambs) 1841; *Layston* 1841-51, 1891; *Letchworth* 1841-51, 1871-1901;
Lilley 1841; *Lt Amwell* 1841-51, 1901; *Lt Berkhamsted* 1851, 1901; *Lt Chishall* 1851;
Lt Hadham 1841-51; *Lt Hallingbury* (Essex) 1851; *Lt Hormead* 1841-51, 1891;
Lt Munden 1841-51; *Lt Wymondley* 1841-1901; *Manuden* (Essex) 1851;
Meesden 1841-51, 1891; *Melbourn* (Cambs) 1841; *Much Hadham* 1841-51;
Newnham 1841-61, 1881-1901; *Northaw* 1841-51; *North Mimms* 1851;
Norton 1841-1901; *Nuthampstead* 1841-51; *Offley* 1841; *Pirton* 1841;
Radwell 1841-61, 1881-1901; *Redbourn* 1841; *Reed* 1841-51; *Rickmansworth* 1841;
Royston 1841-51; *Rushden* 1841-51, 1891; *Sacombe* 1841-1901; *St Albans* 1841;
St Ippollitts 1841-61; *St Paul's Walden* 1841-51; *Sandon* 1841-51, 1891; *Sandridge* 1841;
Sarratt 1841; *Sawbridgeworth* 1841-51; *Shephall* 1841-1901; *Standon* 1841;
Stanstead Abbotts 1841-51; *Stansted Mountfitchet* (Essex) 1841-51; *Stapleford* 1841-1901;
Steeple Morden (Cambs) 1851; *Stevenage* 1841-1901; *Stocking Pelham* 1841-51;
Tewin 1841-51, 1901; *Therfield* 1841-51; *Thorley* 1841-51; *Throcking* 1841-51, 1891;
Thundridge 1841-51; *Tonwell* 1901; *Totteridge* 1841; *Ugley* (Essex) 1851;
Walkern 1841-1901; *Wallington* 1841-51, 1891; *Ware* 1841-51; *Waterford* 1901;
Watton 1841-1901; *Welwyn* 1841-51; *Westmill* 1851, 1891; *Weston* 1841-1901;
Widford 1841-51; *Willian* 1841-1901; *Wormley* 1841-51; *Wyddial* 1841-51, 1891
IGI
England, Scotland and Wales (fiche, 1984 edition)

Watford Central Library, Hempstead Road, Watford, Herts WD17 3EU
Census
1881 census (fiche) whole of Hertfordshire; Middlesex
Abbots Langley 1841-51, 1871-91; *Aldenham* 1841-1901; *Apsley End* 1891;
Batchworth 1841-71, 1891-1901; *Bedmond* 1871-81; *Berkhamsted* 1841;
Borehamwood 1901; *Bushey* 1841-1901; *Chipperfield* 1871, (part) 1901;
Chipping Barnet 1841; *Chorleywood* 1841-1901; *Coleshill* 1841; *Croxley Green* 1841-1901;
Elstree 1901; *Langleybury* 1901; *Leavesden* 1841-51; 1891-1901;
Mill End 1851, 1891-1901; *Nash Mills* 1881-91; *Nast Hyde* 1901; *Northwood* 1901;
Radlett 1871, 1891-1901; *Oxhey* 1841, 1861-1901; *Rickmansworth* 1841-1901;
St Stephen's (St Albans) 1841; *Sandridge* 1841; *Sarratt* 1841-61, 1881-1901; *Shephall* 1841;
Watford 1841-1901; *West Hyde* 1851, 1891-1901
IGI
England, Ireland, Scotland and Wales (excl. Isle of Man) (fiche, 1992 edition)

Welwyn Garden City Library, Campus West, Welwyn Garden City, Herts AL8 6AE
Census
1881 census (fiche) whole of Hertfordshire
Ayot Green 1901; *Ayot St Lawrence* 1841-1901; *Ayot St Peter* 1841-1901; *Digswell* 1901;
Essendon 1901; *Harpenden* 1891; *Hatfield* 1901; *Lemsford* 1851-1901; *Lt Heath* 1901;
Newgate Street 1901; *Northaw* 1901; *Tewin* 1841-1891; *Welwyn* 1841-1901

Appendix VI
Useful Addresses

National repositories
Public Record Office (PRO), Ruskin Avenue, Kew, Surrey TW9 4DU
   tel: 020 8876 3444 (enquiries): <www.pro.gov.uk>
Family Records Centre (FRC), 1 Myddelton Street, Islington, London EC1R 1UW
   tel: 020 8392 5300: <www.statistics.gov.uk/registration/family_records.asp>
British Library Newspaper Library, Colindale Avenue, London NW9 5HE
   tel: 020 7412 7353: <www.bl.uk/catalogues/newspapers.html>
Royal Commission on Historical Manuscripts (Historical Manuscript Commission),
   Quality House, Quality Court, Chancery Lane, London WC2A 1HP
   tel: 020 7242 1198: <www.hmc.gov.uk>
National Register of Archives online index <www.hmc.gov.uk/nra/nra2.htm>
Manorial Documents Register online index <www.hmc.gov.uk/mdr/mdr.htm>
   (N.B. On 1 April 2003 the Commission combined with the PRO to form the
   National Archives and it is expected that it will move to join the PRO at Kew
   at some time later in the year.)

Record offices and other centres
Hertfordshire Archives and Local Studies, County Hall, Pegs Lane, Hertford SG13 8EJ
   tel: 01438 737333 (01923 471333 from area codes 01923 or 020)
   <www.hertsdirect.org/hals> e-mail: hertsdirect@hertscc.gov.uk
   opening hours: Mon, Wed & Thurs 9.30 am-5.30 pm; Tues 10 am-8 pm;
   Fri 9.30 am-4.30 pm; Sat 9 am-1 pm. Closed on public holidays.
Bedfordshire and Luton Archives and Record Service, County Hall,
   Cauldwell Street, Bedford, Beds MK42 9AP
   tel: 01234 228833/228777: <www.bedfordshire.gov.uk>
Buckinghamshire Record Office, County Hall, Walton Street, Aylesbury, Bucks HP20 1UU
   tel: 01296 382587: <www.buckscc.gov.uk/leisure/libraries>
Cambridgeshire County Record Office, Shire Hall, Castle Hill,
   Cambridge, Cambs CB3 0AP
   tel: 01223 717281: <www.camcnty.gov.uk>
Essex Record Office, Wharf Road, Chelmsford, Essex CM2 6YT
   tel: 01245 244644: <www.essexcc.gov.uk/ero>
Guildhall Library, Aldermanbury, London EC2P 2EJ
   tel: 020 7332 1868/1870: Manuscripts section <www.ihrinfo.ac.uk/gh/>
London Metropolitan Archives, 40 Northampton Road, London EC1R 0HB
   tel: 020 7332 3820:
   <www.cityoflondon.gov.uk/leisure_heritage/libraries_archives_museums_galleries/lma>
Society of Genealogists, 14 Charterhouse Buildings, Goswell Road, London EC1M 7BA
   tel: 020 7251 8799: <www.sog.org.uk>

LDS Family history centres

Church of Jesus Christ of Latter-day Saints (LDS) <www.familysearch.org>

LDS Family History Centres in Hertfordshire (telephone for opening times):

St Albans FHC, London Road (at Cutenhoe Road), Luton, Beds
   tel: 01582 482234

Stevenage FHC, Buckthorne Avenue, Stevenage
   tel: 01438 351553

Watford FHC, Hempstead Road, Watford
   tel: 01923 251471

Hertfordshire museums

(please telephone to check opening times before planning a visit; full up-to-date details are also available at <www.hertsmuseums.org.uk>)

Ashwell Museum, Swan Street, Ashwell SG7 5NY
   tel: 01462 742956 : open Sun and BH 2.30 pm-5 pm

Baldock Local History Museum, Town Hall, Hitchin Street, Baldock
   tel: 01462 892640 : open Wed 10 am-3 pm; Sun 2 pm-4 pm

Batchworth Lock Canal Centre, 99 Church Street, Rickmansworth WD3 1JD
   tel: 01923 778382 : open Easter-Oct Tues, Thurs and Fri 10 am-4 pm;
   Sat, Sun and BH 12 noon-5 pm

Bishop's Stortford Museum, South Road, Bishop's Stortford CM23 3JG
   tel: 01279 651746 : closed until 2004

Buntingford Heritage Centre, Manor House, Market Hill, Buntingford SG9 9AB
   tel: 01763 273002 : open 1st and 3rd Sun 2 pm-5 pm

Bushey Museum, Rudolph Road, Bushey WD23 3HW
   tel: 020 8420 4057 : open Thurs-Sun 11 am-4 pm

Community History Centre for Elstree & Borehamwood, 1 Drayton Road,
   Borehamwood WD6 2DA
   tel: 020 8953 1258 : open Thurs-Sat 11 am-3 pm

Datchworth Museum, 9a Datchworth Green, Datchworth SG3 6TL
   tel: 01438 813477 : open 3rd Sun of every month 2 pm-4.30 pm

de Havilland Aircraft Heritage Centre, Salisbury Hall, London Colney AL2 1EX
   tel: 01727 826400 : open 1 Mar-31 Oct Tues, Thurs and Sat 2 pm-5.30 pm;
   Sun and BH 10.30 am-5.30 pm

First Garden City Heritage Museum, 296 Norton Way South,
   Letchworth Garden City SG6 1SU
   tel: 01462 482710 : open Mon-Sat 10 am-5 pm

The Forge Museum, High Street, Much Hadham SG10 6BS
   tel: 01279 843301 : open Fri-Sun and BH 11 am-5 pm (dusk in winter)

Hertford Museum, 18 Bull Plain, Hertford SG14 1DT
   tel: 01992 582 686 : open Tues-Sat 10 am-5 pm

Hitchin British Schools, 41/42 Queen Street, Hitchin SG4 9TS
   tel: 01462 420144/452697 : open 1 Feb-30 Nov Tues 10 am-4 pm;
   1 April-31 Oct Sun 2.30 pm-5 pm

Hitchin Museum, Paynes Park, Hitchin SG5 1EQ
   tel: 01462 434476 : open Mon-Sat (not Wed) 10 am-5 pm

Lowewood Museum (Borough of Broxbourne), High Street, Hoddesdon EN11 8BH
    tel: 01992 445596 : open Wed-Sat 10 am-4 pm
Mill Green Museum and Mill, Mill Green, Hatfield AL9 5PD
    tel: 01707 271362 : open Tues-Fri 10 am-5 pm; Sat, Sun and BH 2 pm-5 pm
Museum of St Albans, Hatfield Road, St Albans AL1 3RR
    tel: 01727 819340 : open Mon-Sat 10 am-5 pm, Sun 2 pm-5 pm
Potters Bar Museum, Wyllyotts Centre, The Broadway, Darkes Lane, Potters Bar EN6 2HN
    tel: 01707 645005 : open Tues and Wed 2.30 pm-4.30 pm; Sat 11 am-1 pm
Redbourn Village Museum, Silk Mill House, The Common, Redbourn AL3 7NB
    tel: 01582 793397 : open Sat and Sun, telephone for hours
Royston & District Museum, Lower King Street, Royston SG8 5AL
    tel: 01763 242587 : open Wed, Thurs and Sat 10 am-5 pm;
    plus Sun and BH 2 pm-5 pm 1 Mar-31 Oct
Three Rivers Museum, 23 Copthorne Road, Rickmansworth WD3 4AB
    tel: 01923 772325 : open Mon-Fri 2 pm-4 pm; Sat 10 am-4 pm
Stevenage Museum, St George's Way, Stevenage SG1 1XX
    tel: 01438 218881 : open Mon-Sat 10 am-5 pm, Sun 2 pm-5 pm
Ware Museum, The Priory Lodge, High Street, Ware SG12 9AL
    tel: 01920 487848 : open Sat 11 am-5 pm (winter Sat 11 am-4 pm),
    Sun & BH 2 pm-4 pm
Watford Museum, 194 Lower High Street, Watford WD17 2DT
    tel: 01923 232297 : open Mon-Fri 10 am-5 pm, Sat 10 am-1 pm, 2 pm-5 pm

Index

Page numbers in **bold type** indicate the principle references to the subject;
page numbers in *italics* indicate illustrations.